Praise for *Gl...*

"*Glad to Be Human* takes a defibrillator to your creative center! It's a field guide to embracing the creativity and spontaneity that bring joy to the business of being human. With an artist's eye and a poet's soul, Irene O'Garden shines her light on the bliss that surrounds us. Each of her essays turns the eye toward love and possibility. I am changed by these now dog-eared pages, and I will return to them again and again for inspiration."

—Annabel Monaghan, author of The Digit series, columnist for *The Week* and HuffPost

"*Glad to Be Human* is a journey of joy. Irene O'Garden has crafted a collection of inspiring, illuminating and vibrant vignettes and reflections that delight and provoke at the same time. Her humor, artistry and love of life are infectious. Whether you read one story at a time or consume the book from cover to cover, you will find insights and phrases that will stay with you long after you put the book down."

—Joanne Sandler, author, senior associate of Gender@Work, former deputy executive director for program and policy at the UN Development Fund for Women, producer and cohost of the podcast *Two Old Bitches*

"In a world that's so challenging and complicated, it's not always easy to remain optimistic. But it is possible. This book reminds us to hunt for light in the darkest places—and find beauty in everyday life."

—Susan Hyatt, entrepreneur, TEDx speaker, bestselling author of *BARE*

"Reading Irene O'Garden's *Glad to Be Human: Adventures in Optimism* is like spending a weekend with your best friend and talking non-stop about everything under the sun. Provided, of course, that you are lucky enough for this best friend to be as wise, witty, thoughtful, articulate, and expressive as Irene O'Garden. Written in an engaging and carefully crafted style that often shades lyrically into prose poetry, O'Garden's essays cover a wide range of experiences, from love and loss, to laughter and living fully in each day. O'Garden explores the essence of what it means to be human with a clear-sightedness that acknowledges pain and suffering while remaining constantly open to wonder, hope, and joy."

—Sheila Fisher, professor of English, Trinity College, author of *Selected Canterbury Tales: A New Verse Translation, Chaucer's Poetical Alchemy,* and other works

"What a joy to read this book! Irene O'Garden's essays are wise and generous, bubbling over with startling and heartfelt insights about our lives and struggles. I kept pen and paper handy to record the many ideas that I want to think about again and again."

—Rosalind Reisner, author of *Jewish American Literature: A Guide to Reading Interests,* editor and contributing author to *Women in the Literary Landscape: A Centennial Publication of the Women's National Book Association*

"This is really a delightful book! Irene O'Garden takes everyday tasks and objects and turns them into fascinating insights. *Glad to Be Human* helped me look around in wonder and find my own delights. In addition to her brilliant text, I loved O'Garden's black and white photos and alluring aphorisms."

—June Cotner, author of *Gratitude Prayers*, *Back to Joy*, and thirty-four other books

"Get ready to devour the offerings at this table set by word weaver and poet Irene O'Garden. Sure, a feast for those who love metaphors, but a banquet, too, for those who prefer the real deal: Life is here for the taking. Love is here for the taking. So take it! This stunning collection of curiosities and illuminations (which I share with my writing students, who marvel at O'Garden's attention to the tiny and ordinary charms in our midst) shows why being human warrants gladness, and with nods to the big and small (A saddleback caterpillar? The Leaning Tower of Pisa?), readers discover the brightest gift of all: gratitude."

—Kathy Curto, author of *Not for Nothing: Glimpses into a Jersey Girlhood* and faculty at Sarah Lawrence Writing Institute and Montclair State University

Praise for *Risking the Rapids*

" 'Family is landscape,' writes Irene O'Garden in her breathtaking memoir, *Risking the Rapids*. She gives us a bold dose of both as she embarks on a remote river trip to help make sense of a family wild and dangerous. In her brave eloquence, O'Garden adds a thoroughly welcome voice to the rich vein of American literature on the singular healing powers of wilderness."

—Florence Williams, author of *The Nature Fix*, *LA Times* Book Prize winner and editor at *Outside* magazine

"*Risking the Rapids* is a deep and powerful memoir. Irene O'Garden sifts through her family's shared pain (and shared joy!) with elegance and care—searching for nothing less than ultimate understanding and supreme forgiveness."

—Martha Beck, sociologist, life coach, bestselling author, columnist for *O, The Oprah Magazine*

"Set aside a goodly few hours with O'Garden's enthralling memoir and plunge into the lives of a family that has chosen you as their new member. Here they are on horseback, immersed in rivers, on tops of mountains—camping, sleeping, quarreling, and forgiving...*Risking the Rapids* embraces our being and never lets go."

—Malachy McCourt, author of *Ireland* and *A Monk Swimming*

"It is a tricky business, navigating the river of forgiveness while honoring the injured self. In that wilderness the psyche must surrender to each boulder life smashes it against, and then stand in awe as we experience the changes wrought within our very DNA that are the gifts of facing down our demons; the gifts of looking our inner and outer truths square in the eye. O'Garden does this better than anyone I know and then puts it into words that have the cadence of angels."

—Linda Ford Blaikie, CSW, psychotherapist and author of
Godless Grace

"Irene O'Garden's memoir is riveting, fiercely honest, and graced with poetic insight. An imaginative child plagued by insecurities, O'Garden vied with six siblings for her parents' approval and lived beneath the Damocles sword of Catholic doctrine. Her chronicle of growing up in what seemed then a normal Midwestern family in the 1950s and '60s asks, 'Who were we, really?' in a far-ranging, haunting journey of discovery."

—Victoria Riskin, former president of the Writers Guild of America, West, author of *Fay Wray and Robert Riskin: A Hollywood Memoir*

"Irene O'Garden's *Risking the Rapids* is, simply put, a literary triumph. Her roiling journey through the whitewater of big family turbulence is alternately a companionable sisterly punch in the shoulder and a vicious left hook to the jaw. And as is true for all superb writing, it is the 'left hook' that unexpectedly provides the narrator's stunning—even transcendent—passage into calm waters and healing. Put aside whatever has gained your attention right now and read this book. O'Garden is truly a wonderful guide."

—Steven Lewis, *New York Times* writer, Sarah Lawrence Writing Institute teacher, author of *Loving Violet*

"*Risking the Rapids* artfully peels back the layers of family to reveal both the darkness and the diamond. O'Garden lyrically shares the challenging circumstances of her Midwest, Catholic childhood as a thread woven through a story of present-day danger during what is supposed to be a simple outing. The kaleidoscope effect of past and present, reflection and struggle bring the reader along on a powerful healing journey to bring what is hidden into the light."

—HeatherAsh Amara, author of *Warrior Goddess Training*

"I haven't experienced this kind of reverberating tension and utter fascination with a family since Jeannette Walls's memoir, *The Glass Castle*. Irene O'Garden's long career of treasured work hits its highest note yet with her memoir. How she survived her upbringing in a big, dysfunctional Catholic family—and the harrowing wilderness trip through whitewaters she took as an adult with her family—is riveting and ultimately healing."

—Debbie Phillips, author of *Women on Fire: 20 Inspiring Women Share Their Life Secrets (and Save You Years of Struggle!)*

"Irene O'Garden is, quite frankly, the most amazing writer I know. She's a poet—just read her words aloud. She's a story-teller—consider the arc of the tale she tells here. She's a dramatist—we're in that boat with her, risking the rapids, and hopefully rescuing our past self as she so magnificently succeeds in doing."

—John Leonard Pielmeier, author of *Hook's Tale* and *Agnes of God*

"Irene O'Garden's *Risking the Rapids* is both a meditation and a thrill ride in which a sibling's death prompts an unlikely family rafting journey through Montana's wilderness. The beauty, moods, and menace of the swollen Flathead River seem an allegory of family life and, like sunlight glinting off water, her brutally honest reckoning is told in sparkling, luminous prose that gives memoir itself a fresh new shape."

—Edward McCann, founder/editor of Read650.com

"*Risking the Rapids* is a sensitive depiction of a family's attempt to heal. In the tradition of classic memoirs like *The Glass Castle* that highlight the coexistence of tortured love and unresolved misery, Irene O'Garden has captured the essence of family connections. With suspense and uncertainty about how complicated relationships unfold, this story intrigues and inspires us. I highly recommend this book to all of us who struggle with the legacies of abuse and the hopefulness to heal."

—Sonya Rhodes, PhD, author and family therapist

Praise for Irene O'Garden's Work

"For many years now, the poet, playwright, and memoirist Irene O'Garden has been a hero to me. I think of her as a walking, writing, beam of light. It is my hope that...numberless others will come to know her gifts and, most of all, her captivating talent for wonder and marvel."

—Elizabeth Gilbert, author of *Eat, Pray, Love* and *Big Magic*

"Bewitching...astounding...heartbreaking."

—*New York Times*

"An immersion into what we relish, how we live, a kind of shining beacon that doesn't shy away from the tough stuff.... Highly recommended."

—Janet Pierson, Producer, SXSW Film Conference and Festival

"In a far-ranging and elegant suite of poems, Irene O'Garden balances a galaxy of incommensurates on the fulcrum of a disciplined intelligence. 'I am a blueprint of a holy universe' seesaws against 'I feel like a set of china'—the former in a Herbert-like sacred meditation, the latter in a narrative about being chased by a bull. Her technique suggests influences ranging from Donne to Bishop, from Frost to Moore. Soulful and rewarding, these poems remind us that 'We're not made of matter but of mattering.'"

—T.R. Hummer, whose poems appear in *The New Yorker*, *Best of American Poetry*, *Harper's*, *Atlantic Monthly*, *Paris Review*, and twelve volumes of his own

"The poems in Irene O'Garden's new book, *Fulcrum*, illustrate the importance and vitality of poetry in our daily lives. Beautiful imagery, powerful emotions, simplicity, complexity and thought-provoking subjects—all drawn from relatable life experiences—make reading her work a journey of discovery and reflection by focusing on what it means to live a life of passion and wonderment. Like the author herself, the poems in these pages inspire and draw one in. This is a beautiful collection."

—Professor Jane Kinney Denning of Pace University, President of Women's National Book Association

Glad
to Be
Human

Also by Irene O'Garden

Risking the Rapids: How My Wilderness Adventure Healed My Childhood

Fat Girl: One Woman's Way Out

Fulcrum: Selected Poems

Women on Fire (play)

For Children

Maybe My Baby

The Scrubbly Bubbly Car Wash

Forest, What Would You Like?

Glad
to Be
Human

Adventures in Optimism

Irene O'Garden

the
tiny
press

Cover Design: Joanna Price
Cover Illustration : shutterstock/ Devon Carlson
Layout: Jayoung Hong
Photos: Irene O'Garden
Author Photo: Mark Lacko

For permission requests, please contact the publisher at:
Mango Publishing Group
2850 S Douglas Road, 2nd Floor
Coral Gables, FL 33134 USA
info@mango.bz

For special orders, quantity sales, course adoptions and corporate
sales, please email the publisher at sales@mango.bz. For trade and
wholesale sales, please contact Ingram Publisher Services at customer.
service@ingramcontent.com or +1.800.509.4887.

Glad to Be Human: Adventures in Optimism

Library of Congress Cataloging-in-Publication number: 2020933892
ISBN: (p) 978-1-64250-246-6 (e) 978-1-64250-247-3
BISAC category code SEL021000, SELF-HELP / Motivational &
Inspirational

Printed in the United States of America

To You,
My Fellow Human.

Table of Contents

Foreword

by Kristine Carlson

Coauthor of the Don't Sweat the Small Stuff...and it's all Small Stuff series. Author of *From Heartbreak to Wholeness: The Hero's Journey to Joy* and *Heartbroken Open: A Memoir Through Loss to Self-Discovery.*

We can all attest to the fact that life gives us our challenges; I've never met another human being to say otherwise. Yet, there's one thing I know for certain, and that is that when we can be present to the small joys and see the ordinary as extraordinary—that's when we are able to keep life in perspective and, amidst those darker days, know that there is a well-lighted path, albeit in breadcrumbs sometimes, to lead the way out of the valley.

Glad to Be Human points the way to having a love affair with your life. Irene O'Garden notices the nuances and aptly shows us her musings through the eyes of gladness.

I love the simplicity of the word "glad."

"Glad" is joy in a softer melody.

It is contentment sprinkled with happiness like a vanilla cupcake with pink frosting—*glad* is the pink frosting.

"Glad" is that feeling you have when your infant stops suckling your breast and returns to sweet slumber after the 2 a.m. feeding.

"Glad" is witnessing something in nature that is a miracle every time it happens—a sunrise and sunset.

Yes, indeed, Irene O'Garden has inspired gladness throughout this masterpiece of creativity.

There are profound lessons in this book, too. Irene shows us the lesson in her poetic depiction of all that seems so ordinary— she brings the simplest concept to life and allows us to be curious about all things.

Glad to Be Human will inspire you to live your most vibrant life—and to keep it all in perspective as you take in these extraordinary passages. It is having a great love affair with life that makes everything livable.

I hope a smile comes over you as you enjoy this book as much as I did and arrive at the same conclusion as me—I am, indeed, "glad to be human."

Introduction

Welcome, dear Reader.

Isn't reading wondrous? Words appear before us and, like the faces of dear old friends, we can't help recognizing them. So it is with feeling glad to be human. We all recognize that wordless, joyous *whoosh*.

I wrote this book to remind myself—and you—how often that shapeshifting grace arises. It spirals in simple moments as we repot our plants, tackle creative projects, or tenderly hang an heirloom ornament. It spreads as we explore other cultures down the street or over the sea. It suffuses us when we witness or perform acts of beauty in the face of our common sorrows.

Our five senses, our fantastic curiosity, our exhilarating emotional capacity are just a few of our avenues to gladness. Even when headlines clamor, or life deals tough challenges, we can find numberless reasons to feel grateful and hopeful.

We humans love to discern and create patterns. It's my hope that this book inspires you to recognize what makes you glad to be human, again and again, weaving and sharing your own brocade of joy.

Irene O'Garden

Curiosities

A Question of Gladness

Why is it even important to be glad to be human? We may be the only species that questions gladness.

This fuchsia-tinted Alstroemeria at my side has no second thoughts about gladly and extravagantly expressing herself.

If cells weren't glad to be cells, could they metabolize? Could they have the little cellular barnraisings that lead to the creation of petals or peanuts or pineal glands?

If atoms were ashamed of being atoms, could they even join atomic hands to make a cell for a while? They'd skip the dance and stay home. *No whirling around tonight, honey. I'm just not up to making a cell. Why bother anyway? I'm not that great at doing it, and after all, cells only die, so why even make one?*

Humans cannot comprehend the larger body we compose, though we can feel its organs in a symphony orchestra, a sports team, a school, a hospital, a movie set. These larger selves need us to function just as we need the beings who compose our bodies. There is great joy when these larger bodies function well, because functioning well is the nature of Nature. Of course, any cell, plant or animal will tell you the purpose of life is not function, but joy. Just ask my flamboyant Alstroemeria.

This coursing sense of connected well-being, or gladness, is the default setting of each living creature, and doubtless, the inanimates as well. (If it's all spinning particles, is anything really inanimate?) The holographic fractal beauty of physical reality is that gladness is important to each, and each is important to all.

Hear Earth purr.

Written in Stone

Broken crocodiles. Lizard tails. Altogether reptilian.
Antediluvian. Elephant skin. Spiral. Wrinkle. Shatter.
Blackened tortoiseshell. In the varying terrain of this wide
petrified flow in Hawaii's Volcanoes National Park, I like what
lava has written.

Blasting sun above, rippled umber underfoot. Ninety degrees.
On our way to Pu'u Loa, a petroglyph site, my husband and
I hike baked lava trail, sanded by eight hundred short years
of footfalls.

Eagerly we go.

Writing always has her challenges. For twenty-first century
writers, challenges are mostly internal: psychological or
time-based. Our ancestors must create both surfaces and
implements before they even start to record experience.

We pick up a notebook, open a glowing screen. They slay
animals, cure skins; pulp plants, layer and dry their tissues. We
buy a marker, a ballpoint. They hunt and excavate pigments;
gather and soak oak galls for ink; find flight feathers, cut quills.
We speak a memo to a phone. They journey with smelly torches
deep into caves; hike barefoot, waterless, over adamant lava
fields to a place sanctified by intention.

We crumple in our tracks. We doubt the worth of our
experience. We thirst for faith in personal impulse. We shame
ourselves with distraction, forget what can be sanctified.

Forty thirsty minutes later, my husband and I arrive at "The
Hill of Long Life," a rise in the landscape, towheaded with
tufty dried grass. A boardwalk rings an area. Fifteen thousand

petroglyphs are carved below our feet. I like what the people
have written.

Spirals. Dots. Targets. Lots more dots. Compelling human
forms. It's said that sailing and animal adventures are told
here. But so many plum-sized dots!

An information board tells us parents traveled here in hopes of
ensuring long lives for their children. Each "dot" was carved to
cup an umbilical cord which was then covered with a rock. This
hill shimmers with wishes.

Those who flourished returned to carve their stories, and their
wishes. I love this old human impulse to inscribe, to write,
to leave a mark. Whatever the challenges. I like what hope
has written.

Peace.

Free Sample.

Cleared for Take-Off

Like dust. Worse. Like rust on my desk: two or three months'
worth of unprocessed paperlife. Not bills, you understand—
all the really urgent stuff got done. But filing and questions
and forms. Matted, as ever, with perfect excuses: travel,
performance, submissions, and family and friends.

(Not only that, but here in the Age of Distraction, we have
hyper-super-ultra-extra other ways to duck and cover.)

Pussyfooting around my desk, I thought I was postponing
discomfort. Truth is, I felt it every time I entered my office.

Once I faced that heap of indecision, I found two funny pockets
of irrationality. First: *Stern verdicts are called for: imprison
things in the file cabinet or slay them in the wastebasket.*
Seated at last, sorting and tossing, I smiled. Silly fear, as if
letting paper go is letting go of people or events. As if memory
were made of paper.

*But clearing the desk feels like a waste of creative time. I could
be making something new!* Rust eats whatever is beneath it. A
desk is space for new creation.

Making space is never a waste of time, just as making time is
never a waste of space.

The shadow side of our wildly entertaining Age of Distraction
corrodes our Age of Satisfaction. But with a bit of inner elbow
grease, we are cleared for take-off.

There's always time if you do it now.

Domesticities

Taking the Plunge

Near our little house in the woods runs a lovely rushy stream, Clove Creek. While it's often brisk and prosperous, it takes a huge spring thunderstorm to understand how such a modest flow could carve out the dramatic and beautiful area known locally as The Gorge.

The Gorge is right across from our three acres. Hemlocks veil the approach, but cooler air and the sound of dashing water draw the visitor to a stony path between two handsome maples. The path shortly opens to a massive outcropping of rock and The Gorge itself.

Here, Clove Creek—tumbling over boulders over centuries—has carved sheer rock walls, blue with lichen, graced with fern. The most vigorous waterfall narrows through two huge rocks and creates a swirling pool some twenty feet below an immense stone promontory. It's a place of remarkable power and beauty. Dag Hammerskjold summered nearby, and often could be found on this great jutting jaw of rock, gazing down at the falls.

It used to be a rite of passage for local teenage boys to leap off The Rock into the cold pool, but with the abscess of insurance rates, the owner got crabby. He took to calling the police to chase the hoodlums off.

For nine years I'd been saying to my husband, "One of these days, I'm gonna jump off The Rock myself." No small aspiration for me, considering my last game of Neat Falls.

Neat Falls was a backyard game invented, as far as I know, by my older brother. He would start as The Judge, packing his Daisy Air Rifle. He would then shoot each player one by one (or "pick 'em off," as he liked to say). The object of the game was to stage the "neatest fall," that is, the most realistic, exciting or gruesome death. The winner got the honor of becoming The Judge and shooting everybody else.

Although I'd taken it in the gut many times and writhed in what I thought were truly excruciating and lifelike deaths, by the age of seven, I had yet to be The Judge.

One hot Saturday I'd had enough. I resolved to make the coolest, the bravest, the very Neatest Fall of All, one that had never been conceived, much less attempted, by the older kids.

Our backyard had two areas, the upper part for baseball, Neat Falls and other games, and the sunken part, where the swing set and sandbox were. An eight-foot wall of pebbly cement marked yard's end. Every spring a dump truck in the alley dumped a fresh load of sandbox sand over this wall.

It's true that one or two of the braver desperados had gone to the last round-up from this wall, but in sissy ways: a slow crumple and fold, and an inching grapple downward. No drama, no propulsion.

When my turn came that day, I waved everyone down to the wall. Heart pounding, I went through our garage to the alley and stepped on to the wall, with my back to The Judge.

"Fire!" I shouted. The bullet sears into my back. Do I crumple and turn like a coward to fall forward? No! With a cry of anguish I fall backward, down, down, down seven feet into the foot-high mound of sand, thud. All the wind knocked out of me. Neatest Fall Ever Accomplished. Rotten thing was, my brother didn't agree with me. He gave The Judgeship to one of the Archibald boys.

Jumping off high places stayed on my list of high-risk, low-gain activities, until I heard the first screech and splash of a triumphant adolescent at The Gorge. If they can do it, I can do it, I thought to myself. It was a pleasant nugget to carry on my walks, stepping out onto The Rock in all seasons with the knowledge that someday I would step off it into space and whirlpool. This vivid picture entertained me for almost a decade.

Then we began our search for a larger house. My days by The Gorge were numbered. I took other, milder risks—a barefoot walk in a nearby marsh, a naked moonlight swim in a neighbor's pond. The summer was drawing to a close.

I was reading on my porch one warm evening, my husband out of town, when my friend Jane drove up with a guest in her car.

"Meet Rainbow Weaver," she said as she got out. "She's in town to give some workshops and I thought she'd like to see The Gorge."

Abundant and radiant as a full moon, Rainbow Weaver rose out of the car. Jane had mentioned that a Native American wise woman was coming to town, but I never expected her to be so young. She was not long into her thirties, if she'd gotten there at all.

She had a firm handshake and a ready laugh. As we chatted, I sensed her natural reverence, but there was not a somber bone in her body.

"Shall we walk to The Gorge before it gets dark?" asks Jane.

"Sure!" I say, always happy to show it off. "You know, I'm gonna jump off The Rock one of these days."

"Nice night," says Rainbow Weaver, looking at me with a wry smile.

"Well, who knows, maybe tonight!" I chirp nervously.

This walk, always so soothing, acquires an unfamiliar edge. I might actually have to do this.

In no time we arrive at The Rock. My eye screens little movies of my foot catching on the way down, lacerations, Mr. Crabby calling the police, a severely broken—

"Beautiful spot," says Rainbow Weaver. She drinks in the power of the hemlocks, the stone, the falls, lit by patterns of setting sun. Her gaze rests on me. In her eyes I meet my own desire to do this thing.

"Well, I just might jump tonight."

"If you do it tonight, you'll have witnesses."

Something I'd never considered. The Jump is instantly more appealing.

"Never be a better time, I guess," I say, with a knocking heart. I strip off my cotton skirt, leave on my tank top and underwear. Rushy blood. Metallic taste of fear. I'll pluck up my courage with a thanking chant to The Rock. I compose it on the spot. "Thank you for the gift of courage, Brother Rock, Brother Rock. Thank you for the gift of life, Mother Earth, Mother Earth."

Rainbow and Jane join me on the choruses. I am marching around rhythmically now, close to the edge, girding my loins, careful to thank and bless each nature spirit and my own body and my witnesses—

"You just keep making up verses, don't you?" says Rainbow.

I pause to defend myself but at once I know she's "RIGHT!"
I shout. With a pumping leap and an animal yell, I plunge
off the rock, down, down, deep into the icy water, down and
down, never touching bottom, then pulling up and up, bursting
through the surface, exhilarated, splashing, whooping like a
joy-drunk child.

Rainbow Weaver was a wise teacher. From those brief
moments in her company I learned many things about
approaching risk: to observe myself without judgment, to keep
a sense of humor and a light touch, to invite witnesses if I wish.
Most important, there comes a time to stop approaching a risk
and take it, letting desire propel me.

As I paddled deliciously round in the pool, I found I hadn't lost
Neat Falls after all.

Perfect or not,

here I come.

Charmed, I'm Sure

Which comes first, the chicken or the charm?

We loved our little old farmhouse, set in the woods, my first garden. A charming nest of creativity. Plays, movies, poems, calligraphy, books, even my performing literary magazine (*The Art Garden*) was hatched there. Crystals amplified our energy. Pure streams of belief in creation flowed.

Yet when we had six to dinner in our booklined baby dining room and one felt the call of nature, three guests had to stand to offer access. Bedrooms small as twin beds were our studios, so overnight guests folded up on the fold-out couch. A beloved jumble. But after five years, even our muses were crowded.

We began our hunt, not knowing quite what we wanted, knowing we would know it when we saw it.

I had a dream one night of a fascinating, satisfying, three-floored house, where I ascended the top flight of stairs to see a sign that said, "Welcome, Writer." Out the window I saw artists working on the house, colors ribboning.

Three years into our search, we found a stopgap dream house. A pond, a place to walk the dog, quirky rooflines. We could take this wall down, this could work. Road a bit too busy, house a bit exposed, but this could work. We make an offer. The owner accepts. We exchange homebaked pies.

Just as our giant complex wheels of financing began to turn, we were crushed to discover she took a weekender's cash offer. Didn't even call us. Tears in our eyes. How could she lie with a pie?

Two more years we spent crumpled in our little place, climbing into the realtor's red Audi at a moment's notice, wincing at houses peculiar, claustrophobic or badly sited, wrong for all kinds of reasons.

One day our realtor called. "I have a house to show you. I warn you, it's revolting."

"Great, Matt. Always interested in seeing a revolting house."

We were first to see it on its first day on the market.

We still laugh at shelter magazines and their guides to selling your home: *Plant a few flowers. Scrub down your house. Paint it white*, I read. Whenever we showed our house, I baked cinnamon bread.

This house smelled like ten cats and ten-year-old litter. A patina of filth filmed the walls and the scummy shag rugs. A child-sized turd perched in a bathtub. Still, scruffy-stuccoed, scraggled, we knew at once it was the house for us.

Sunlight wept in relief through the row of French doors. The carved bird above the fireplace, paralyzed in paint, had not fully lost her voice. Peeling walls and wires and the mucky littered basement did not dim this building's native grace. Meadows opened like peripheral vision, taking in wild turkeys, redtail hawks, the rising moon, the sound of church bells. I felt like Vita finding Sissinghurst.

Early the next morning, I rummaged through my little studio. How to claim this house? I found a tiny cube of Japanese stick ink. Ink. Perfect symbol for two writers. I tied a narrow slate blue ribbon round it, slipped the midget gift into my pocket.

We met the realtor at the house at noon. Away from his eyes, I palmed my inky charm, slid it to the back of an attic closet shelf, claimed the house in full belief. Happy hearts pounding, we put in our bid.

Two days later, we got the call. Our bid had been accepted.

Click of heels and clink of glasses! Gosh, that charm worked fast! But next day, a call from our accountant drew our celebration to a screeching halt.

"You could squeak on through, but I think you really want to sell your house before you buy this one. Just to keep things comfortable."

Shoot. We thought we had a hold of the house that had a hold on us. It felt so much like ours. Tail between our legs, we made the call, withdrew the offer.

Back on the market it went. We had to sell and couldn't speed the process. Months went by. No matter how many bouquets I set out or loaves I sugared, we couldn't charm a couple into buying.

But every so often, and on every major holiday, we found our way to the lane of our hopeful house, as close as we could get without trespassing. We stretched and bent to glimpse it through the tangled hedgerows, peering through the prickly barberry at the grounds, the house itself transfixed by a woebegone, cobwebby, sleeping-beauty charm, cast by the troubled family who owned it.

Inspired, perhaps, by the Top Hat, The Scottie, The Roadster—charms of the real estate board game—each time we visited, we brought a little thing to bury, to remind the house of us. A little ring. A jigsaw puzzle piece. A couple bulbs of daffodil, one to plant near the catalpa, one on the wild hillside. Other trinkets, now forgotten.

The stick ink stayed planted deep in the house. *Give off rays, Ink. Give off roots. Keep anyone from buying this but us.*

An entire year went by. At last, the people destined for our farmhouse found it. The day their financing came through, we made the breathless call.

"Is it still available?"

"They've shown it for a year and no one else has made an offer. They've slashed the price a third. It's yours."

Wheee!

Was it the charms that did it? Yes and no. Charms are outward nuggets of intention. Emblems of focus, channels of desire. The power to create or attract what we want is not in the objects, but in the verbs, like *desiring* and *intending* and *believing*. But I do love the cozy little nouns, those playful symbols that make hope physical.

The story could have ended there, but doesn't.

After fifteen years of working on the house, freeing it from its sour spell detail by detail, the inner camera pulls back to reveal the house as a larger charm on a bigger board, another Monopoly piece.

For if a charm helps you manifest a needy house, the next thing you want to do is manifest good people to work on it. Then you want to create the best working situation for them and encourage their creativity. You want more than a lovely place to live. You want to be the kind of person you'd want to work with.

The person you aspire to be. That's a big game board, and fun. And you're not the only one playing.

The bigger charm channels not just our hopes, but those of the gifted artists, designers, builders, gardeners, stoneworkers, keepers who hold and fulfill their own visions for the house, for themselves as creators and us as cocreators.

Like our cube of ink, a house, or a job, or a school, or an art form is not an end, but a means. A means of expanding and expressing feelings and aspirations for ourselves, for one another and for beloved physicality. Which *is* charmed, I'm sure.

Imagine a way in rather than out.

The Nature of Niches

When we were creating our kitchen, the question of tiling in the back of the stove arose. Bulging cornucopias and della Robbia opulences and painted little Quimper figures are available for such kitchen landscapes. Since the shelf-life of tile is nearly eternal, we pored over choices. I finally realized no matter what we installed, after years of standing and stirring, I would tire of looking at it.

But what if we could renew the view? I proposed a niche, for a shifting display of art. So, as the saying goes, we made a niche for ourselves.

It's just a little tiled seven by nine inch opening cut into the back-splash, off-center. Ironically, art rarely shows up there. It belongs to flowers, which I change almost as often as the menu.

In a world where we're told to carve our own niches, or find our niche market, we're often advised to keep doing the same thing to fill that niche. But why display the same inert behavioral cornucopia? The ultimate nature of niches is space for a change.

A Sign of Gratitude

In a dusty, dim antique shop in a semi-shuttered upstate town, a jutting corner of red caught my eye. I slid out the stained wooden sign from behind the eyesore table lamp. "YAD-OT." It pleased me immensely instantly, this smooth, hand-crafted piece, even before I got what it said. And then it pleased me even more.

The old salt at the desk told me it dates from the '20s or '30s. He got it from a printshop on Varick in Manhattan which created signs for movie theatres. Indeed, there was another sign that said "yadrutaS stratS" but this was the one for me. After all, how often is its subject advertised?

The other day, our handyman hung it in the kitchen above our pantry door, where we can see it daily. But later, when I shut the door with some vigor, the sign jumped off the wall, narrowly missing my head. "A fitting end," I thought with a smile.

Yet I have been granted another and yet another "YAD-OT," and I am full of gratitude for the gifts each brings. The sign dove off the wall so I would remember to share it with you. (It now hangs securely in a quieter place.) May you be filled with joy and multiple signs of gratitude. And may you enjoy each and every "YAD-OT."

Meaning appears

in response

to our attempt

to grasp it.

Geographies

A Visit to Liberty

First, the souvenirs: Copper Lady, Plastic Lady, Lady in the
Snowball, coinbanks, cedarboxes, thick and tasseled pencils,
placemats postcards mirrors spoons cups metal paper rubber
bear her blue image. Also fries dogs shakes.

Buy our Admit Ones from the whitehaired grizzlejawed joe
sparkling under his cap. A short wait, then board our red white
and blue tidy ferry.

Stamping children, flappy flags, ziz of nylon jackets. Every
size jeans, polyesters, gold bridges, camera necklaces, not just
Americans, but Citizens of Everywhere.

Hair of every kind streaming over faces. Chiffon scarves
fluttering, fluttering. The violins within my blood begin to rise.

Thickhand men derope our boat. The Hudson flushes under us.
We're off.

Grey and black and navy hugely tower. The pier disappears as
we peer at the flannel and seersucker buildings compressing.

Hoisted like masts in the brisk ferry air, we squint through
sun-and-spray-tugged lashes. Teeth dried by windward smiles.
Fluttery cheeks. Ferry bottom slaps on the river's knee. Part of
a sandwich flies by.

Old fort, gunhouse, then Ellis on the right. Pink brick sinks in
my eyes. My stomach says in another life I knew that place,
off the stink of the ship chilly chilly damp harsh pulled shoved
cursed, named another name, I embraced my partly hideous
destiny. Kindness was not yet popular.

Bright oblongs, slices of light, sun punctuates the water. City reduced to a pattern of blocks, gull-garlanded.

◇◇◇

And there, as silver and as green as juneborn leaves, she twists. There she grows now, so tall, the tallest woman you have ever seen.

Yes, you can even look under her armpit. What a great big holy face! The boat is tipping, cameras clicking.

The beacon herself welcomes us. Green goddess in the harbor, bearing light and knowledge. Her grotto is the open sky, the water is her shrine, appearing to the faithful with dignity divine. Grave and peaceful, calm and holy, she stands at the nation's door.

The ferry slows, the ramp swings down. A hundred faces wondershown: awe, delight, craning necks, clasping hands, chewing gum, lug the sliding baby, rumpled pamphlets, shrieks of laughter from the girls. Chiffon scarves fluttering, fluttering.

Rubber legs on terra firma. Up steps and steps and steps, wide grey group steps.

Lighted displays in the pedestal, sepia photographs—not now! not now! To the top to the top!

Black and many stairs, wrought iron. We are not in a building, but a woman. Race to the top to see whom she attracts.

Gigantic folds of gown softly corrugate the space. Look, there's the book, that's the torch! We are up so high my body is reverberating. My thighs retract my knees.

This single skinny black steel rail spiraling out the orangelit green is all that holds me from downward spiral. That, and absolute knowledge I will not fall. Death is offered us in many moments. We refuse it every time but once.

I do not even need the rail.

◇◇◇

Lady Liberty, Lady Liberty, who's inside your noble face? We whirl in your brain, Lady L. Here in her head, we are Liberty's dream.

Gaze at the green horizon. See the hazy town. Glide with the garbage barges. Green grass patches all round.

Look past the reedy reaches of New Jersey, past silver green of Pennsylvania, to brown leather Ohio, shouldered Indiana, waving birch of Illinois, deep green corners of Wisconsin, to the blue and white of Minnesota, my home state, North Star State, crystal star state in my heart, my brow. Hi Mom.

Like a deck of cards, Iowa's corn goes by, Nebraska's grassy bluffs, sweet virile Colorado, patient glory of Grand Canyon and blur-rimmed Mojave. Neon jazz of Vegas and the fertile crop of Hollywood. Lady L., we know you from your miles of movies: cruise movies, crime movies, sailor movies, city movies, comical pastoral, historio-tragic. Here in your head, like favorite actors, boys dare each other with their elbows. Girls imagine swandives.

She changes the world in massiver ways than she knows: greeting, forgiving the restless arrivers: all those hearts crying for new starts. *The journey is worth it*, she says.

This Lady knows peace: *Peace*, she says, *is activity with love.*

Full of white blue pink cloud thought, descent is a twirl of
honey onto bread.

◇◇◇

Quieter voices and feet emerge through a fabric of stimuli:
bleep of the giftshop register, sneaker squeaks, noisy boys: "If
you dropped milk cartons off the top, they would crush your
skull." Girls squeal and shake the globes. Their elders flip
brochures and pocket money.

Oh, those sepia photographs.

Rows of workers sweating over steaming vats of bluing starch
soap. There in the red case, heavy black iron, heated by fire.
Hiss on the wet shirt.

Much unchanged since sepia-time: dedication, patience,
singlemindedness, the body's praxis of routine, nights of
reflection, exhaustion and fear—

Yet, stepping on the ferry with a wearied immigrant, we share
a brimmingheart smile. Stepping on the ferry at the feet of
Liberty, glowing in her halo, we remember we are free.

We jeans, we jackets, in the open air free and open to each
other now. We are Liberty's dream, and Liberty dreams
the world.

The girls are flinging giggles overboard.

We are free, as the use of our eyes, free as the gulping air, free
as the chiffon scarves fluttering, fluttering over the waves.

THE PLEDGE OF ATTENTION

I pledge attention

To the flow

Of the United States of Consciousness

And to the Reality from which it stems:

One notion

Of our Good

With liberty that just is for all.

Idiosyncracies

Bless This Mess

A mess has a visceral effect, doesn't it? Monday morning, I ground my coffee, filled the coffeemaker with the ordinary amount of water, went into the kitchen to cook the oatmeal and returned to an unsettling sight: bulging sopping grounds overflowing the basket, spilling onto the counter and clogging up the coffeepot itself. The body draws back as if from a startled silverfish scuttling in an empty bathtub. A mess is a little scary.

Messes have a bad reputation. A mess isn't really scary. It's just a mess.

There's nothing like a mess to abrupt us into action. There's an order we like to return to. We come squalling into this world, making some particularly unpleasant messes we are unable to remedy ourselves. And all of us have suffered the wild parental screech, "Clean up your room!" But growing up is about finding an increased tolerance for, ability to make and to remedy messes.

Sometimes in cleaning up a mess, you make a bigger one— the set of strainers, pitchers, and auxiliary carafes needed to strain the coffee grounds and capture the brewed coffee filled our sink.

But there's something lively and life-affirming about a mess. We can't help responding to it. We can ignore it hereafter, but it still exists and we know it.

Part of what's scary about messes is that sometimes they can make us feel as if we have done something wrong, which makes us feel bad.

In the case of the coffee, I had done something wrong. I had been a little too generous with the grounds. (No, I do not measure, I eyeball. I would rather deal with the occasional mess than measure out my life in coffeespoons.) Overfilling the filter meant that a few fellows floated up and over the paper, slid down the cone and plugged the driphole, which made everything overflow. If only I had had my coffee before attempting the operation, I would have been so much more alert!

Of course, we're always thinking we should avert messes. But a mess is not a judgment Nature makes. Even a volcano, arguably a great mess-maker, simply creates another landscape, another arena of possibility for new life forms.

Some messes mirror us, reflect where we are internally, which is generally not in the present moment, to which the mess kindly recalls us.

Really big messes, like hurricanes, unite people like blood cells: white blood cells to remove the unusable; red blood cells to rebuild.

Some messes are nests of indecision, like piles of paper. Sometimes it's hard to tolerate messes. But that's a prerequisite for any creative endeavor. Mixing bread dough one day, I became conscious of this. There is a stage in making no-knead bread (a fabulously simple recipe to be online) where flour and yeast and salt and water are ragged. You stir and stir to eliminate this as if mess and mistake were one. But they are not synonyms. All this mess is a stage in getting from ingredients to bread. So perhaps the messes of our lives are stages in the golden loaves we are becoming. Which go pretty well with a cup of black coffee.

Having a Cigarette

Emerging from a stressful time a few summers ago, while on retreat, I decided to take a walk to the lake. It was a lovely evening. I had anticipated seeing the lake, but not planned beyond that. Along the soft strip of beach, a lounge chair lay open in white receptivity.

But I am an accomplisher. I don't just sit and look at a lake. Too reed-choked to walk the circumference. What was I to do, walk back? Bathed in late sunlight, the lapping lake coaxed me to stay.

I was cast back to childhood. At a moment like this, my mother would sit and have a cigarette. So that's what I decided to do, lean back in the long white chaise and have a cigarette. Without the cigarette. As I sat inhaling the evening, I thought of breaks—coffee breaks, smoking breaks. It's not so much the coffee or the cigarette, but the break itself. The break for pleasure.

Addiction is convenient, since you don't have to decide your pleasure—you don't actually have to pay any attention to yourself at all. But convenience is expensive—it can cost your life. Or at least many dollars.

Substance or not, becoming aware of the pleasure in the present, the ongoing fulfilled promise of existence, is ever an option. Even an accomplishment.

Practice Life-o-suction.

Demittere Diem

The other night I suffered a thigh cramp. A real howler—when muscles gang up on each other and each, in defense, grips all the harder.

Sucking deep breaths, I can't answer my awakened, anxious husband. Bending, leaning, rotating. Coaxing, begging the leg, which snarls and defies like a mad dog.

Isn't this over yet? Stop. *Stop.* And it *won't.*

In spite of the eternity pain stages, it doesn't last forever. Eventually our flailing finds alignment. Try good leg. Foot ankle thigh take weight. Shift to ailing limb. Acceptance! It is relieved by the weight, glad of normalcy and, in its sheepish canine way, apologizes for its lapse of muscular sanity.

I'd vigorously exercised these muscles earlier. Shouldn't they be tired and want to sleep? Yet, as body will, they'd been mirroring my frame of mind.

For I'd been pumping my muscle of accomplishment just as vigorously. So much to do, to see, to create: Christmas cards, gifts, errands, visits with friends and family, making house sitter arrangements, having contractor meetings—all clamored to be done. We'd booked substantial renovations for the following several weeks and planned to travel while the workers slung their power tools.

Carpe Diem (Seize the Day) is the very motto of our age and has inspired me plenty. But, our thighs remind, if we seize non-stop, we seize up.

So here's my little corollary: "Demittere Diem" (Let Go The Day).

Returning to a daily taste of yoga helps me do same. As does looking at an unretouched sky. After all, the vigorous and mighty sun does it every night. With style.

You can travel faster than the speed of light,

but it will be dark when you get there.

A Personal Holiday Tradition

Christmas: so many words, so many details, so many packages, so much food, so much laughter, so much love. And, for me, the child-angel: a little glitterworn ornament who has graced every Christmas I remember. I never heard her story, but perhaps it goes like this:

My frosty-breathed parents, taking in the holiday lights on a freezing Midwest night. One hand securing his fedora, Dad slides his other arm through Mom's. She wears the big-collared green coat she loved so well. (*He pulled me to him by that collar and said, "Betty we're getting married."*)

There, in a thirties shopwindow perched this little musician on her shiny star. Dad goes back the next day for it, surprises Mom on Christmas morning with this happy hint of the children they long for.

The angel takes her Christmas place as the babies are born, ornaments four lonely-needled trees in a row while my father is at war. In the stylish fifties, she could have looked cornball, but instead retained her charm. Jetson-era, while I made jazzy silver-sprayed table-trees of Styrofoam balls and toothpicks, she was not threatened in the least. Other ornaments came and shattered or aged poorly, but high in the branches or low, hung to the front, or hung to the back, she hung on.

When Dad passed and Mom sold the house, I retrieved this little Ghost of Christmas Plastic from the estate sale box. For some years, she hung year-round as part of a wall grouping I made with an old parasol and some sheet music.

Eventually she went back to her seasonal appearance. And perhaps it was she who inspired me some years ago to begin a personal holiday tradition.

When it comes time to trim the tree, we make a point to give thanks for a special blessing with every ornament we hang. There are always new blessings to give thanks for—creative efforts, new friends, trips and so on—but certain ornaments evoke specific thanks each year. The red cardinal is always for John's mom. The seashell strung with golden rickrack hangs for coastal friends. And this little angel always seems to sum up the season's best and oldest truths. I hang her here today, in thanks for you, gentle reader.

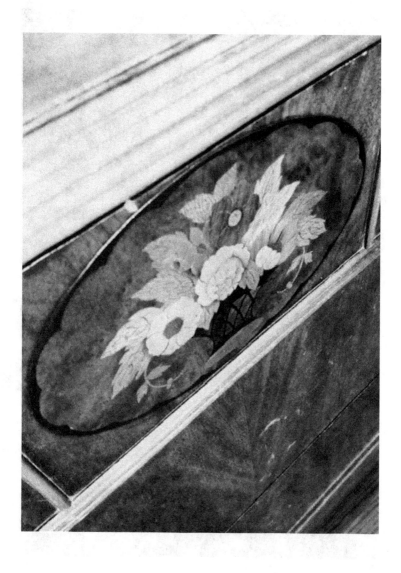

Intimate Furniture

Spared the junk heap: a chest of drawers, a mirror and a lamp. Swaddled in plastic and cardboard, freighted cross-country to us at the request of my sensitive husband. Intimate furniture, this.

Chest with a delicate marquetry nosegay, lately relieved of my lonely sister's glut of grim novelty outfits, she herself lately relieved of her loneliness, finally now, at the memory home, where she sleeps in its matching nosegay bed, with the match to this just un-bubblewrapped crystal lamp.

In deeper previous days, chest, lamps and mirror are proud possessions of my namesake great aunt. The bureau: a home to her silk slips, society sweaters. Home to the pearls at the base of her goiter. Mirrored. Home of adornments and longing. Intimate furniture, this.

Sensing it now before purchase and lacquer: a cabinetmaker's affair. Love of wood and of work spelled in matching veneers, glowing in torches of wood grain. Topped with the shapely frame he carved and bent, glue drying, till the day he slipped the glass in and beheld himself, maker of his own image.

One grieving day, the bed and chest will reunite, the crystal lamps will find each other. The mirror gathers new faces in flashes, adjusting appearance, emotions. The chest receives the sift of peachy powder, the moustache clip, the sprouting grey. Intimate furniture. Every humble meaning stored behind the glass, within the drawers, by the unconditional light of the crystal lamp.

"Don't change"

is all we cannot ask for.

Tending Pleasures

I keep close track of the fruits of age. The joy of tending is
one of the juiciest. Some come early to this appreciation
(parents especially), but as a rhapsodist of creativity I came
late. For years it escaped my notice that tending is actually the
foundation of creation.

The early will-based verbs of youth—exploring, creating,
acquiring, establishing—can harden into nouns in middle
age: expansion, mastery, collection, accumulation. In age,
these pale next to the nearly parasympathetic verbs of tending
and releasing.

In age, we learn to tend what we have and who we are, and to
release that which we cannot tend whole-heartedly.

We recognize the old shapeshifter Need will rise again and
again, but that her shapeshifting sister Tend is always at the
ready: to oil the thirsty wood, to weed the bed, to soak the
ragged cuticles. To read to the child, to help with the move, to
work the phones, to clear the rubble.

Need and Tend, Need and Tend, great systole and diastole of
our human heart, unified playing field of life in all her forms,
colossal pump of love.

To learn to love in every circumstance is maybe why we came.
To learn that love itself needs tending and tending is love itself.

Botanies

Root Truth

If you looked closely as I slid the rootbound plant out of her pot, you could actually see my guilt woven into the gnarling nest of roots. It's been so long since I last repotted my houseplants that a botanical welfare agency was bound to track me down, charge me with neglect and cart them all away. I did consider giving them to someone more attentive, yet the orange Clivia offered a blossom of patience and forgiveness, even as she sat atop the perfect root replica of her pot.

So, with relief and pleasure, I set to it yesterday.

One gift of physical labor is the embodiment of metaphor. My thoughts from this pot were obvious—dwell on your roots too long, you run in circles and take up all your growing space.

But as I worked with various roots—hairy, lumpy, milky, airy— truth came up my hands.

We associate roots with the stagnant past, but they constantly seek the new—new water, new nourishment, new exchanges. They are the probing present, which sustains the past. And the future as well.

Every July we think about our family and our nation's roots. It's good to remember they need repotting occasionally, too. After all, root is a verb.

Our souls became American to choose.

Ridiculously Tiny Trees

When I was younger, I regularly drove by a wooden fence where someone had planted fifteen little spruces, each just the size of your hand. "Ridiculously tiny trees," I'd think to myself.

These were the same ignorant years when I'd page through a garden catalog and say, "I'm not planting an apple tree. You have to wait too long for it to bear fruit." Took me ages to realize that whether you plant or not, five years will pass just the same. Either you'll have apples or you won't.

But who doesn't love massive graceful old trees? When we moved into our present house, we were awed by a stately allée of century-old catalpas. There were also towering cedars, mighty chestnuts, and grandmother dogwoods shawled in lichen. Testament to the long view of the first tenants.

Yet no mid-sized trees. A whole generation of trees was missing. Fascinated by dogs and horses, the intermediate owners ignored tree planting. We brought along some Arbor Day babies, which are mailed as pinkie fingers. The crab and hawthorn now blossom and fruit and shelter the birds. We've planted many other trees as well, including a reserve of catalpa offspring to replenish the allée when the time comes.

Now, in the company of old trees, I'm always on the lookout for the young. It's a comfort to see them springing up in Central Park or along the Taconic or the Palisades Parkway. And those fifteen spruces? They are taller than I am. Whenever I pass these teachers, I gush with affection.

We sometimes embark on adventures feeling ourselves as tiny trees, indeed. But it lately occurs to me, that if some things are too big to fail, nothing is too small to plant.

Learning curves.

Quizzical Squash

Home from our trip to find on the leafy vine in our nearly past-
tense garden a half-my-dog-big cloudy blue Hubbard squash.
Quizzical. Knobby blue globe, swollen with summer sun and
rain. A thing that almost doesn't seem like food. Food rarely
asks an ax in preparation.

You can see how someone thought up bowling. Such a
wonderous thunderous squash could rumble Rip Van Winkle
skies, knock the ninepins down. Quizzical, though. How and
when can this become a dish without a lumberjack to whack it?
And a baseball team to eat it?

You can't accurately at the moment call it squash, since it won't.
Squash, that is. Not yet, anyway. Not till the mallet and cleaver
reveal two seedy buckets to be scooped, till the turkey pan and
long lazy roasting turn it from its fierce Formica form to a soft
sweet heap. Squash is the very endest product of itself.

Yield of my garden, I yield to the impulse to look you up, be
certain of your Hubbard-ity. Yes, the images are all this smoky
slatey shade. Many are wartier, oddly ovoid or elbowed. In
fact, I now appreciate my shapely one, you fat blue toy top
of a squash.

But I'm not in the mood to eat squash today, and my upper
body's too fatigued to tackle it. One writer says to bag your
Hubbard and to drop it on the floor. But it gave me all
these words today. I have affection for it and that seems
disrespectful. Quizzical. What shall I do?

I turn to Alice Waters on my shelf. She always has an answer
and today she says a winter squash is better left to sit a few

weeks after harvest. I'll wait for the orange of October to open this blue. Maybe you'll join me then, too.

Vegetables and fruit

love human contact.

Muguets and Tissues

Oh, the fuzzy muzzy muddle-headed mediation of a cold! Right
in the middle of this scurrying season, the flow of life congeals,
senses blanketed in thick subterranean retreat, Jell-O in the
veins and brain.

Though people come and go throughout your day, forget your
appearance—nothing makes your puffy self attractive. Red
rims every feature of your face, your cracking voice seems
to be emerging from an antique bathosphere, and the few
movements you care to make are like a stop-motion animation
with the motion mostly stopped.

But there is comfort in withdrawal after a week of intense
effort. And perhaps at day's end, you can, in your pajamas,
gather sorrel from the garden, roast garlic and shallots, chop
the last potato, sip that savory soup, steep your ginger tea,
climb into bed with an old-fashioned whodunnit, blessed by the
faint but detectable scent of a nosegay of muguets you plucked.
And that's nothing to sneeze at.

Sprung

Though momentarily concealed, the sun was out long enough this week to bless the dining-room bouquet, soften the earth in the garden and distribute a general feeling of relief here in the Hudson Valley.

Help arrived yesterday and busted up the last crusty, recalcitrant, gravel-studded humps of snow, scraped away the tattered mats of autumn leaves, and leveled all the yellow silhouettes of "winter interest"—those grasses, rosehips, desiccated flowerheads we leave in the bleakened landscape to lift our hearts.

Snowdrops, crocuses, green poking spears—all the lovely little spring clichés bring comfort, for I'm wrestling with the angel of an old writing project. Caught myself thinking that finishing it will be quite an accomplishment.

But that approach can be a winter of its own. Does Nature "accomplish" spring? Is it a list of tasks she checks off one by one? When she's finished, does she collapse in a cloud and say, "Glad that's done!"

Those poking crocuses remind us creative projects are not sets of tasks, either, but living things, with their own seasons, growing out of ourselves into themselves and at last, springing free of us.

Process = Progress

Startle Display

After a week away, I could hardly wait to get fresh flowers in the house again. Michaelmas daisies are at it this time of year—starry blooms in fruity purples, chalky periwinkles—and the glorious shrub (*Lespedeza thunbergii Gibraltar*, or bush clover) is at the height of her beauty. Her long stems are crowded with opulent, pea-like blossoms, and if magenta can be gentle, she's it.

I happily loaded my gathering basket, but ouch! Felt something sharp as I clipped her stems. Almost like thorns, I thought. How uncharacteristic of the pea family.

Indoors, I began arranging the stems in a vase.

"Ow! That really hurt!" The heel of my hand went red and throbbing. I picked up a leaf.

Talk about startled. The tiny animal looked like an intergalactic visitor. I promptly googled it. I had been stung by a saddleback caterpillar. Who knew there even were stinging caterpillars?

If defense were the ultimate expression of power, saddlebacks would rule—they are the most well-defended creature I've ever laid eyes on. Those multiple spiraling spines are not only sharp, but venomous, and can break off and lodge in the sting-ee. The spots that look like a big face are meant to scare aggressors. Boo! It's called the startle display.

When you calm down, though, and look again, you see this fellow is essentially an armored slug, just trying to get his naked, vulnerable self from here to there. He grows up to be a spikeless, venom-free furry brown moth.

It was worth the sting and startle to behold this creature who reminds us fierce defense is but a passing stage in growth.

Coincidence of Rarities

As plants go, it's an eyesore. Scarred, scallopy, leathery, lesioned leaves all akimbo on the bony stems. Three hundred and sixty-four days a year, that is.

But some unpredictable summer night, a prehistoric, dinosaurish scaly head lifts from the troubled leaves and opens to a melon-sized, pristine, fragrant wheel of glory. It is the legendary Night-blooming Cereus.

A paradise for moths, a silken tunnel of immaculate complexity—this opulent, ephemeral wedding of a flower has inspired parties for centuries. (We've held one or two ourselves.) As we left for Canada, we noted the swelling buds and resigned ourselves to missing this year's display.

Yet our lumpy friend reserved her two spectacular blooms for the very night of our return. As we sat in admiration, the waxing moon set early, leaving a dark starry stage for another annual rarity: the Perseid meteor shower. No haze, no clouds— for the first time in several years we could watch the thrilling, erratic archery of shooting stars.

The shooting stars: quicksilver blossoms. The cereus: a slower shooting star. Unity in rarity.

Geographies

The Smudge Between the Stars

The evening news burst into our imagination: a possible "Comet of the Century!" Comet ISON, discovered in December 2012 by amateur astronomers, was expected to appear in the late November night sky, brighter than the moon itself! A whoosh of memory followed like the comet's tail: the ache for and the arc of wonder that propelled us to the Everglades to witness, maybe the most famous of them all: Halley's.

Hail ye, Comet! Blasty, sunbright Comet! Cast my shadow on the boardwalk; flatten me against the cypress. Weak my knees and knock me over. Blow like a TV car crash in the constellations; make it impossible to sleep for the writing of long letters to great-grandchildren describing blaze and arch and movement over the rattan welcome mat of the draining Everglades.

Just in case, though, we bring along binoculars.

Over the marsh on boards, twelve strangers trod. Up then the wide, wood tower where bird eyes swoop the flat, eyestretching land.

We've come to see, but seeing's not the point. The point's to feel the low, slow note: a wavelength seventy-six years long: *Halley's Comet.*

An hour to wait. The sun goes down like cellos. Compass to be *sure* that's west. Ibis fall asleep. Twilight. Time of promise.

Twelve yearning toward the stars, weirdly fearing—despite the bellclear night—the stars will not appear.

On this broad tower, this porch, this dancefloor of an observation deck: an older vigor-couple, a mother tightly ponytailed, her teening daughter, a crinkle-eyed matron with two daughters and their men, two college boys, and a scruffbeard photographer.

Charts, guides, trivia aside, seeing's not the point. The point's to feel the ancient round vibration.

Up into friendly space we look, where humans now have set their feet. Over the great leaf sea of the Everglades, ancient craft sail by these ways.

Squeal of the first star found. Dodge feasting mosquitos at their comet party, drinks on us. Birdcall tumbles from a large beak. Men talk and study charts. Women lean and huddle.

Star by star, night fills. Star to star, eyes leap zillions, quillions, drillions of miles. Twelve forms: a silhouetted jury sways in starlight. Photographer's binoculars scan like radar.

"Think I got something!"

Excitement ricochets around the tower.

"Where? Where?"

Rustle of feet across wood.

"See Jupiter, then those stars there? Right next to that one."

"Where? Where?"

"Gotta use the binocs."

"Where? WHERE?"

He makes a papernapkin map with ballpoint stars. There, by
the three-star curve, through chubby lenses I behold: a smudge
between the stars.

◇◇◇

The Mighty Comet is a fluff. A blur. A tailless bit of lint. A scrap
of tattered papernapkin. Dandelions gone to seed are showier.

"Oh, Harry, we came all the way out here for that?"

It *is* there.

Entirely unstarlike, uncelestial. Mistake of a shaky God. An
optical whisper.

Seeing's not the point, the point's to feel. Feel what?

Bone-shiver. Sense a yellow afternoon just after recess,
counting up the years till seeing Halley's Comet for myself,
feeling blessed to be living at the same time.

Bone-shiver. Sense Calusa and Tequesta, Seminoles and
Englishmen, Chinese, Babylonians, Mark Twain himself—this
smeared astronomy, these black glades teem with centuries
of witness.

Bone-shiver. Sense my body recollecting herself as light:
surging, centerless energy meeting, crossing bits of ice and *we*
became a comet.

Perfect strangers. Each a wonder, aching for wonder. Sharing
flashlights, lenses, observations, in the wonder of perfect trust
in a dark swamp under the starfull sky, the sky, like Earth,
where nothing is too subtle or too small to love, where majesty
is masked in smudges, cells, in us.

Some joking, some sagging like popovers, two by two descend the steps.

Out under the billioned sky:

"Good night! Great seeing the comet with you!"

Voices echoing over the Everglades.

"Least we can say we've seen it."

New zodiac appears.

"Good night!"

The comet glides above, away.

Decades later, Comet ISON tantalized. But we have since learned that beyond our Earth, our Jupiter, beyond our very Neptune, a shell of such smudges surrounds our solar system. We are swaddled in comets. A blaze of glory would have been redundant.

Creativities

A Pocket-Sized Mystery

One wintry day I took a walk in nearby snowy fields. I called my older sister. She was in a friendly phase of Alzheimer's, and I knew I could give her a definite moment of glee describing the snow. She's overjoyed she never has to deal with it again in San Jose, and relishes every opportunity to say so.

After our conversation, as I put away my phone I felt a long thread inside my jacket pocket. I snapped it off and was about to throw it on the ground to let it biodegrade, when the thought arose that perhaps a bird would find it useful for its nest come spring. This field was ringed with tall spent weeds. I chose one close to hand and dangled from its frizzy head the long blue thread.

Who knows if it will survive the winter blasts, I thought. But if it should, it might prove useful to a fellow creator.

I went on my way a bit longer, then turned around. Dreamy winter mists were rising from the snow. A good day for a picture. I reached for my camera, scanning the scene with photo eyes.

There appeared to be a white bowl floating deep in the brush. Too far into tangles and thorns to get a good shot, but it looks to be—yes—a nest! A nest with a single fat egg of snow. Nice hello from the universe, nice thank you from the birds. Delightful to feel such awareness at work. I'll try to capture a picture.

Stepping back to frame it, I glimpse a wisp of teal. There, directly in line with the nest, dangling from a weed head, the very blue thread I had hung for the nest builders!

I walked around to the other side, to look at my first approach, to see if I had seen the nest subconsciously, but it was entirely obscured by thick weeds, branches, tangles, and saplings. It was as if the nest appeared the moment I hung the thread. Or the thread flew to the weed the moment I noticed the nest.

Such pocket-sized mysteries are present whenever we're present for them. A gift of inward retreat, when we let go of accomplishment and just pay attention.

The events of life

illustrate its text.

Questionable Qualifications

Dylan is the latest in the succession of canaries who've graced our lives—Whitman, Basho, Vincent and Oliver, all named for poets. (Since only male canaries sing, Vincent and Oliver commemorated Edna and Mary.) Dylan came to live with us near the hundredth birthday of a certain Welsh poet, who kindly lent his name to our bright musical fellow. Dylan adjusted immediately to his new digs and began singing promptly the following morning.

Such a voice is a great cheering sound, especially as winter comes in. Makes me think of how we came to get our first canary.

I grew up with parakeets. I never even heard a canary sing until, in eighth grade, I visited a friend whose mother had a glowing beauty in an elegant cage. His song was celestial, something out of *Bambi* or *Snow White*, but it all seemed out of my league.

I grew up, moved to New York and we got a parakeet. But on my way to my waitress job, I'd pass a pet shop in the underground concourse of Rockefeller Center. Canary song glorified those echoing halls.

I'd come home to our parakeet and peppy as the little squirt was, I remember saying to myself, "When this bird dies, I'm going to get a canary."

I'd hear his sweet but squawky Damon Runyon voice and look forward to liquid canary song—until one day I listened to my own ridiculous voice. Why do I have to wait for him to die to get a canary? Who says you can't have both at once? I laughed out loud. We became a two-cage household.

Since then, I try to listen for the scratchy, squawky qualifications I unthinkingly impose on life. Releasing silly limitations lets the heart sing.

Birdseed

when planted

does not grow birds

but when eaten

does.

A Cherished Mistake

In my late twenties, I heard a Robert Shaw Chorale recording of an early American folk hymn, "God Is Seen." It so strongly moved me that I went to an artists' colony to illustrate it.

I prepared for a month—studying visual literacy and the color wheel, carefully planning and sketching twelve 16 x 20 inch images. At last I mixed my watercolors and joyfully, confidently painted all twelve on luscious Arches paper. The final touch I planned was to apply narrow outlines using a pinpoint nib and India ink.

If you know the delicate crowquill nib, the toothy surface of French coldpress watercolor paper and the ineradicability of India ink, you know a perfect collision was waiting to happen.

It didn't have long to wait. The moment I put pen to the first painting, shocking black spattered all over it, spoiling the image.

I was overcome, I was nauseous, I wept. No undoing these black blotches. The splatter was too extensive, the ink intractable. I was crushed. More than one painting was ruined—eleven others had to coordinate with it. A month of work wasted! I was furious. I felt punished. This was a book about God, for God's sake!

I finally calmed down enough to hear my only solution: "Pretend you meant to do it."

I grabbed my toothbrush, the ink and the pen, practiced spattering on scrap to see possible effects. Then I intentionally spattered all twelve. Suddenly the paintings were dynamic, their texture and energy newly alive.

If I could have hit "delete" at the first spatter, would I? You bet your sweet art I would have. But this visceral experience taught me lifelong respect for the spontaneous in art and in life. While I love our world of deleting with so much easily erased or rearranged, there are rich lessons in things we can't undo, in discovering how to abide, appreciate or even cherish them.

Don't let your talent

kill your creativity.

No Masterpiece

I had the privilege of seeing a David Hockney retrospective. I was eager to see his work, because when I read that Hockney was creating art on the iPad, it had cinched my decision to buy one.

It was deeply nourishing to see an artist creating so exuberantly at seventy (though it's silly to say, since I'll be there myself in a few short ones and I intend to do same).

Gallery after gallery, Hockney's bright, affirmative spirit emerged in dashing forms: trees, leaves, flowers, hillsides—a feast of shape and color. Giant paintings made of six or nine or thirty-two joined canvases. Big exclamations.

In one densely hung room, among dozens of watercolor sketches and corresponding oils, my eye singled out a small painting. On closer examination, I was surprised to discover it was not a particularly strong composition. No outstandingly deft use of color. A middling painting. Nice enough, but not breathtaking. No masterpiece.

Hockney has sustained some criticism for the varying quality of his work. But as I looked and questioned, I realized that what drew me to the painting was an awaiting insight: creating a masterpiece was not Hockney's intention here. He was responding to what he felt about what he saw. Seeing such a quantity of his art, such a multitude of his responses made that clear to me.

We as artists, as humans, are not called on to create masterpieces. We are called on to respond and to record our responses as honestly, thoroughly and exuberantly as we can.

Whatever form our responses take, each time we do this, we get better at it.

To make a masterpiece, we must first be a master anyway. If we do "master" an art, it is because we return to it again and again, asking more of it and of ourselves, in service of what we are trying to express, not of what we are trying to become, or how we are hoping to be regarded.

We can all become masters of expressing ourselves.

What absorbs you again and again? What would you say you have mastered? For me, it's spontaneity.

To Makers

If it matters to you,

It doesn't matter if it doesn't make money.

It doesn't matter if it doesn't make sense.

It doesn't matter if it doesn't make headlines.

It doesn't matter if it doesn't make friends.

It doesn't matter if it doesn't make things easier.

It doesn't matter if you don't know what it is.

It doesn't matter if you don't know where it's going.

But it does matter.

It doesn't matter if it seems obvious.

It doesn't matter if it seems silly.

It doesn't matter how it seems.

You do not matter how you seem.

You matter how you are.

It doesn't matter if it comes easily.

It doesn't matter if you struggle with it.

It matters if you don't make it.

It matters if you don't make it matter.

It matters if it bothers you.

It matters if it makes you laugh.

It matters if it makes sense.

It matters if it bleeds.

It matters if it makes you cry.

It matters.

You matter.

You make it matter.

You make it.

You make.

You.

The Birthing Tent

Just beyond the nimble Frisbee dogs, a flapping sign guides crowds inside. Although I assisted at my sister's labor, my husband's never seen a birth. We join the broad-swath demographic: marshmallow-sneakered grandparents, glittered tweens, toddler-straddled dads, miles of mothers edging their excited offspring to one-day, two-day, three-day chicks, stinky red piglets, tawny Mama and her calf born only yesterday. Below fumy fists of spun sugar, smells of straw-strewn mud and manure seep up deep behind the eyes, unlocking species memory, cave wall.

We find a spot on the bleachers. People clamber up around us. Shoulder to backpack, ten-deep they ring the aluminum rails, tiniest frontmost. Only this far away from us, her big spotted body sways.

"She's young. It's her first," says the hickory-haired man at the mike, in the chambray voice of generations of animal husbandry: creased with experience, softer than laundry. "We ask you to please be quiet."

For a moment, people are. Hundreds hear her blowing, watch the heaving bellows of her ribs.

"Mommy, will she have her baby now?" chirps a voice beneath a giant panda.

"When she lies down, then she's ready," says the hickory voice. "We're all waiting for that." Behind him, a knot of people—a woman and four men—hook their pockets, scuff and murmur, check the vet kit.

Little by little, a whine, a marimba ringtone, escalating buzz of conversations. *Is it worth it? Should we stay?* Parents phone spouses. Oh, people, people. *Shshh!* runs round the bleachers.

This show has no starting time. Always a flow of new viewers, a noisier jockeying herd.

"She about to have it?"

"Naw. May be awhile," mothers tell arriving mothers.

"Look, there's a baby calf born yesterday," they say, to distract their restive young, and come to think of it, some mothers have no need to witness, given their first, how tough it was, how long it took. As a matter of fact, "Let's meet Daddy at the Midway."

We're staying put. People jostle us, stand up on the bleachers, block our view, remind us we are glad to have no children.

"Cows gestate nine months, like us. She's a Holstein and they're dairy cows. Meant to be bony and thin, not muscled like beef. If you see a fat one, she's unhealthy." He scatters bits of information like feed, keep us ruminating while we wait. "We call them heifers till they have their first, then we call them cows."

Twenty minutes in. Tail switching, she shifts, starts down. Seems her moment has come. Ripples of excitement. But no, she uprights, circles, sways, moans, trying to be comfortable.

If we are patient, we will be just in time.

Forty minutes in. Again the gentle voice tries to quiet the half-replaced crowd of newly piping, griping children, elbow-bumpers, shufflers and shovers over bleachers. It's not happening yet, change the channel, out they drift. It's only birth.

The team stays way behind the rails, beyond the reach of questions, studying their fingernails. None is comfy talking public like the hickory man, the voice of farm itself, calm, reassuring, but farms need more than voices. Their eyes, their hands, itchy as sailors heading out.

Still the shifting crowd, the shifting cow and still we stand.

She bellows, rolls her eyes, and nearly kneels. The crowd gasps, and yet she stays upright. We feel her boulders of discomfort, the immensity of her burden and her youth.

Shhhhhh spreads round the crowd, committed now. Committed to wait, to help with observation, hope, to model quiet for those who forget.

The moment she starts to kneel, motorcycles start a few tents over. Who planned this tent arrangement? Oh people, people.

An hour in. She shifts decidedly, and down she goes. Cheers, applause, flashing cameras.

"Ladies and Gentlemen, please be quiet."

Her motorcycle-punctuated labor torques in earnest now. She twists and bawls, eyes oscillating fear and trance of birth.

Stringy swinging mucous. How can that barely distending entrance release a baby cow? This is birth? This happens every day? Other mothers lead their young away.

The vet slathers his gloved arm with lubricant, calmly massages her, and inserts his arm to the elbow. Very quiet now. He gently feels around, gently pulls out. Flips a soft word.

The Voice tightens slightly.

"Calf is big and it's her first, folks." Deep breath. "We're going to help her out."

She's in trouble and the trouble goes on as they don work gloves, align themselves, prepare the chain. Piercing, foaming, bloody trouble. Not insulated by pixels or cathode. She thrashes in the sodden straw. We all taste the salt of her pain. Why is coming and going so hard for mammals?

She is young but trusts the careful crew, doesn't fight the vet who reaches in again to shift ninety pounds of calf stuck inside her womb, to wind the chain, to bind the cannon bones above two unborn pointed hooves and shield them so they will not tear her on the way out.

Then the signal. One and two and three and four people pull, pull as a single strap, a human sinew.

No good. They release. Breathe. Shake their shoulders.

One, two, three, again they pull, with all their thewy bodies, pull from the dug-in heels of their boots, the only parts of them touching the ground.

Still no good. An inch of ease-up on the chain, but no pause, no breath—no time—only biceps, chests, backs, thighs quivering with the added weight of shock that it isn't over yet, pulling back now, nearly level with the earth, a single straining muscle of might and will, faces running with beautiful deadly concentration, and that, not the cow, is the picture I want and do not take.

The pointed hooves, the head, the sudden blue splitting membrane, huge slimy calf ejects at last, tumbling the pullers. Tears, cheers impossible to contain are hushed.

"A little heifer," the voice says, low as a golf announcer. "Just what we hoped for. Normally they don't—" but now we are looking at the vet, who is pounding and pounding the calf, as if he's administering CPR. Which in fact he is.

Taste the iron memory: life can do this. Sometimes knowledge, effort, care and focus, hope are not enough. Children can be watching. Sometimes people take a Thursday summer outing to cuddle up to Nature, and it ends a sodden lump on a barn floor.

Today, though, the calf jerks and sneezes. Someone hands the vet a hypo. Another swabs iodine over the navel. Someone holds a nippled bottle of colostrum to the sucking lips, while the dripping mama lurches to her feet. She turns, smells, licks her little one as if just a summer storm had passed. Oh people, people.

A page

is a friend

beamed backward

and forward

in time.

Why Write

Words, dependable as the rising sun of day, bear mysterious images, shying out of my forest, learning to trust me. I feel their breath, their lips on my palm.

Welcome to my clearing. I will care for you.

Some are exotic, with towering iridescent plumage, or gleaming spotted hides. Others are humble, shrew-sized grey furs streaking over my forest floor. They tame me, too, to calmness, patience, openness.

They take me from the world of time, from the snipping and fitting of activities, the piecework of deeds. *Live the long flow,* they say, like wide, wide, windwaved wheat in the sun from horizon to horizon.

Each image brings a present. Often it is wrapped in questions, set in the moment like a plant in dirt.

They invite me, some, to ride upon their backs, and I do, to feel the mighty charge and change of galloping muscles beneath me. Some, mostly smaller ones, ask me to become them, and I do, feeling the flapping of webbed furry wings, or the dance of the multiple legs. Then I may ask, "What's to be done?" They answer only, *Ride, ride, and be, be.*

So I lie down and some of them lick me like a block of salt. I see I too am something for them. Others begin to nibble, and it does not hurt at all, it tickles. It feels warming and appropriate and others now are taking bigger bites, they are devouring me, these images, and it is such an act of love. Lush washes of feeling formed by the pleasure-woven wisdom of the earthy eating way one must pass to know the truth: we are beyond our eaten bodies, we are a mist of knowing, selves without cells, awareness itself, cascading through innumerable bodies, we are the wind through the wheat in every way and each of the ripe heads blowing.

Geographies

Paris: A Literary Truffle

Before my first trip, my friend Jorie said, "Paris is all it's cracked up to be."

Now after dreamy walks & mist, tassels of surprise, glitterings, gleamings, shatterings of color in the fresh baked streets, blare & quietude, advance, retreat, the anticipated delicacy of ordinary days well-fulfilled, fine French faces crinkled in welcome, I know it's true.

First Things First

From the bottled airplane air we emerge into the peculiar techno-dream of Charles de Gaulle airport, which is this: After riding ascending conveyor belts, you are discharged into a roulette wheel. You bobble around by chance, circling, circling the endless crowded circumference until, without information or arrow, you bounce down the proper chute to the exit.

We emerge at last into genuine air. Grogginess dissipates, pierced by the tang of arrival.

◇◇◇

The friendly taxi driver starts the first of many gracious conversations we will have in Paris, where with touching courtesy and respect, he speaks English and we speak French. He refers to a garden we pass as a "zoo for plants."

He turns down a very quiet side street on the Left Bank and spots the gently swinging sign for our hotel. At nine in the morning, our room isn't ready, of course, but we'll drop off luggage. We pass a life-size marble angel and potted figs into a cobbled courtyard.

Our hotel is a former convent and its serenity lingers amid the potted boxwood, the urns of impatiens, and the stone lions, all harbored by ivy-scrambled stucco.

The staff is as polished as the great front desk. They greet us warmly and say the room will be ready at three. We look around. The woodpanelled parlor, with its honor bar, features several well-colored belle époque portraits, smartly unframed. Their intriguing faces suggest a sip of Dubonnet, a bon mot or two, a whiff of scandalously fascinating private lives.

◇◇◇

First to Notre-Dame. Her intricate sandy façade opens into a dark, mammoth incubator of prayer and reflection. We spiral up stone stairs to gargoyles, rooftops and the dim raftered loft holding her great holy bell. It hangs simply, gigantically, unfenced, uncaged. We lean for a closer look. A persnickety guard barks, serving as velvet rope. Through a tiny door we wriggle from the shadows to the dazzle of the Sunday sun on the cramped tower walk. Beyond the narrow parapets, Paris in all her centuries lies ruffled at our feet.

Bonjour, La Tour Eiffel! The sight of her insouciant straddle is more infrequent in Paris than expected. At the end of a side street, we glimpse her iron knee, and are off like hounds on a scent. Reaching the rolling wide swaths of lawn at her feet, we flop down like Dorothy and the Tin Man and nap on the grass in the sun. Name another major landmark where one can simply fall asleep. Too tired to tour La Tour, we didn't even get to her toe that day.

◇◇◇

Next, to the haunt of Stein and Joyce, Hemingway and Fitzgerald: Shakespeare and Company, hub of twentieth-century literature. As dim and bibliodorous as an old bookstore should be, chockablock not only with books (in English), but the residue of itinerant writers. On the upper floors, sofas and cots wedged among the serried shelves are by night nests for the struggles of literature. The walls are tacked with manifold well-worded yellowing thanks. A black pillow of cat opens an eye in our direction and, world-weary, turns away.

For a while, we inch along the streets with a guidebook written in dull detail, with a voice like a boring old architect uncle. Finally, sleepily realizing we have no obligation to the book, we abandon it and let Paris talk.

Wrought iron balconies spill geraniums. Awnings glow. Broad limestone buildings repose in morning sun, graced with faces, swans, acanthus. Well-muscled stone bridges curve over the river as naturally as arms from shoulders. A crooked little pea-green house with paprika trim squats at the end of a lane. Any minute a crooked cat will slip out the bright door chasing a crooked mouse.

We find a corner boulangerie and sink teeth into the first crunch of true croissant.

Meandering through the streets, our first sidewalk café on the Rue de Buci, tracing the steps of an old friend who came to Paris in her teens in the heyday of the sixties and strolled the streets barefoot, with a white mouse on her shoulder.

A pushy street musician installs himself over our onion soup. He has the bad judgment to play nothing French, only songs we hate, which another pushy musician plays at our local Mexican restaurant in the States. We always tip the man in the Mexican restaurant, but here we harden our hearts to "Besame Mucho" and the player's bad breath. He tries to convince us with his shocked expression that we are the only people who have ever refused him money.

Eating Monet

After a day or two of rest, we are ready to dine.

The waiter steps out the front door to cough.

The waiter carries a long dark platter gently as a baby. He stops at our table. With a slight bow, he ceremonially proffers the fish. And introduces us.

"This is the white tuna you will be having. He has been slowlyslowly grilling all day," he says. His manner implies, "This is my generous friend whose company you will enjoy." He returns him to the kitchen to be sliced.

Strudel is brought to a neighboring table. The waiter slices the shattering crust. A few morsels fall out. Knife & spatula in perfect accord, he removes the entire delicate pastry counterpane, lays it gently aside, and deftly drops les petits morceaux back in proper alignment. He smoothly replaces the top. It never happened.

"La grand-mère du chef," answers the waiter when we ask who is framed on the wall by the kitchen door. "Une dame précieuse," we smile. She loved roasting, he tells us. We behold her. To roast is to bend and baste; yet she is chine-erect in her dotted dress. Head held proud as a suckling pig's. Curls white as lamb frills. Eyes full of juicy opinions. She gave the boy her culinary rectitude: attentiveness to living food. The chef is present in his kitchen every night.

A woman enters with her schnauzer, meets her friends at table.

A brilliance of salmon on crisp, dissolving pastry. An egg delivered upright in an eggcup, cap of the shell sawn precisely as if by diamond cutter. Within, a light poached yolk nestles in its whipped white, baptized with sherry vinaigrette.

A man at a nearby table is dining alone. He photographs each course as it arrives.

A bowl of tomato intensity, gazpacho bite delivered by an oval of mustard ice cream. Ravioli of date, sweet onion, cumin, warmed in nasturtiumed seafood broth—the pasta a mere idea holding it together. Returning to the salty Breton butter and the crisp wheaty baguette again and again, grounding ourselves on earth, then sailing into each dish.

Noses in magazines, the couple next to us discusses decoration.

We are lost in the melt of mussels, the grilled truth of tuna, the butter of cheese. Tears in our eyes at perfection. "Nous pleurons, monsieur, nous pleurons," we tell the waiter. He smiles.

The chef opened the meal with a dab of caviar mousse on a delicate pastry; he closes it topping the same fine pastry with a pale pool of mint glaze.

We try to word this experience to ourselves—these cloudy and vivid washes of pure flavor. "Eating Monet" is as apt as we get.

Foiling Pickpockets

Another day, not far from Notre-Dame. Clustered on the pont with a small crowd, watching a living blue fairy. She has alighted on an overturned black box, her private stage.

Her movements are precise and slow and as otherworldly as a praying mantis. Gently fluttering gauzy bat-ish wings are looped to her splaying fingers, making the air a part of her. Her face is smeary cobalt blue streaked white and gold and is inscrutable.

A nudge at my backpack. My New York nerves prickle. Someone has flipped one magnetic catch. The two buckled straps on my dressy city backpack are fake-outs and he didn't fall for it. For convenience sake, my valuables are elsewhere on me. My heart thumps not with worry, but invasion.

I turn. The pock-marked youth who nudged me will not look me in the eye—he pretends to be absorbed in the fairy. Not even a pretend look, a pretend apology for "bumping" me.

For a moment I hear his damaged face. Handsome thieves are only in the movies, Madame. Handsome has other ways to make a living. No one will look at me, so I lead a life where I intend they shall not. His dirty thumb has left a mark on the fawn-colored strap. We move on.

◇◇◇

Strolling with John in soft drifts of people along the old Seine barge track. A man close behind me. A press on my backpack. I spin. "What is it?" asks John. "I don't like people fiddling with my backpack" is my testy reply. The man melts away before I can look at him.

◇◇◇

Paris Est Railroad station, 6:30 a.m. An hour early for our train to Switzerland. Burdened with baggage, we sink into chairs at the indoor sidewalk café. We order tea, yawn, talk. No prickles

or sense of invasion this time, just the sight of two hands on my
backpack atop the luggage six inches away from my right hand.

"MONSIEUR!" I shout. The hands withdraw. I know no words
for this, no French curses, but anger finds an international
voice: I start loudly growling like a dog.

He gets the message. I watch the tall form unhurriedly depart,
as if he'd missed his train, but knows another will be coming
shortly. Later I spot a pickpocket casing the streaming crowds,
watching not the people, but their bags. No doubt his second
baseman has an eye on him, waiting for the signal.

Les Petits Plaisirs

Tiny gardens, squares tucked throughout Paris like silk pocket
handkerchiefs. Flower borders like bolsters of brocade line
the walks in the Tuileries, Luxembourg, Jardins des Plantes,
upholstered in shock-shimmer colors under the pale plane
trees, against tall packages of yew. Starry firm flag-like patterns
claim the eye, assertive as living remarks.

Long vistas to buildings. Space for consideration, space
for appreciation. Space to breathe, almost Japanese in
the sensibility that one needs what is not there in order to
appreciate what is there.

Ruins in corners everywhere—piles of broken ornament moat
the Louvre. Cracked stone crowns slouch on rose-flecked walls,
crumbled cloister bones scattered by the giant Chronos. Pearly
light coats rooftops, chimney pots. Swooping swallows.

Pouring rain, sudden sodden chill. Long-sleeved shirts, layering
a short-sleeve shirt over a short-sleeve shirt under a long-sleeve
shirt for warmth. Sipping steaming chocolate.

Sacred Shock

Touring churches for their starry ceilings, smoky paintings, twisted pillars like groves of trees behind the altars. We swing a church door open to the sight of a coffin on six shoulders. Gaspily remembering the point of churches: art for life's sake.

A building is like a head. Plenty of wall: a solid skull protecting all the processes; windows: the outward eyes.

The sacred shock of Saint Chappelle is that your own cheekbones are replaced with stained glass to your temples. Your face stays put, but jaw to crown around your head turns to panels of colored clarity. As if brain had wings, as in a dream where you find your house has rooms you didn't know about.

This pavilion of colored light soars upward sixty-five feet in the air. It is like being within a dragonfly's wing, or inside a multiplying dragonfly eye, airy, the power of flight assumed, indeed, *assured*. Angels grinning with the carver's certainty of heaven. A space built to honor the Crown of Thorns becomes a crown of light. My head did not know it could be that tall, but it carries the knowledge now, returning anytime to stand kite-minded in that faithmade space.

◇◇◇

After the three o'clock tour with the Paris sun sieving itself into pure color on the patterned floor, feeling God's light on your own face, we spot a poster for a chamber music evening of Les Russes in Saint Chapelle that very night. Yes. Tchaikovsky might help express it.

Returning at night to the dimmer, star-glimmered space. Prim chairs laid in lines over the marble floor. Electric candles.

Inward reflection, quieted colors. Murmuring audience.

The Chamber Orchestra enters and bows. An engaging
ponytailed grinning violinist speaks. He indicates the players
with his bow: a tall, bashful, dark-haired young man clutching
his violin; an ivory-complected serious young brunette, violin
red against her black frock; a stiff, square-built matronly
teachery violinist who looks as if she'd rather play in private; a
big rubberfaced seen-it-all double bass player; and the balding
cello-shaped cellist whose eyes reflect the taste for sorrow
cellists always have.

Eyes on ponytail, they commence at once and joyfully, all
nerves channeled into the ache of the Russian heart sung
through their strings, flooding with yearning the venerable
space and the chambers of listening hearts.

Sitting in the front row we watch as well a concert of
friendship—signals, commencements, encouragements
flowing between their bright and watchful eyes as easily as
notes. Watching players play, we remember that music is
such agreement, such work, such concentration, such trust
between, as the scaffoldings that held the carvers and the stone
cutters and those who placed each bit of colored glass in these
darkened windows. Churches and music are proof of what
humans can do when they believe in the nameless, themselves
and in others.

A twang rang through them all as the string broke, flying up
to the startled teachery face. Blushing, confounded, she leaves
the stage like a nurse called to duty. Seriousness descends.
A little death. She left. We thought she would always be
playing with us.

They try to play as if the wheel had not come off, as if the stone in the shoe were not embedded in the arch, as if their sister were not sick. Sound thinned, the empty voice of worry counterpoints. Measures and measures later she returns, new string secured. Their eyes brim welcome and relief, as do all of ours. Her face, unused to smiling, smiles. The broken string has fused us all into Tchaikovsky, who, full-throated, fills the hall.

D'Oeuvres

Time only for a few hors d'oeuvres of the great feast Art in Paris, but chefs-d'oeuvre they are.

The great swooping sheeted Winged Victory. The lush hypnosis of Impressionism. The Venus de Milo whose body fairly breathed but who should have lost her head. "Oh, if I must," we heard the artist sigh in stone, begrudging us her face, stiff with his indifference.

The tall halls, the acknowledgement of centuries of human effort. Stone people, arrangements of paint. Music on the steps, drums on the bridges.

"Go at night," said the guidebook. Of a late Thursday, we went to the trashed spot. Wrappers, napkins, programs, maps sullied it like litter at a carnival. The book was right. Only three or four other people there. We could stand right at the railing and gaze for ten undisturbed minutes at the geisha of changeable serenity, the living sepia intelligence, the compelling simplicity of form and complexity of expression. Time without nudges, space without elbows to search her face for answers to her own mystique, to be, as Leonardo was, looped in the loops of her hair, to wonder as we leave the Louvre what other painting had held us ten minutes asking.

Père Lachaise

Black doves. Angels bearded with years of city soot. Bits
of colored glass. Famous names. The rainy old cemetery, a
little city itself: houses, grottos, temples, towering trees, part
peaceful, part embattled.

Carved torches, trampling horses, stone swords swung in an
endless siege against Death itself. Granite banners. Ferocious
battle cries against Forgetting, caught in marble throats. The
din is almost audible. Strange artillery: basalt blocks like tanks
blackly insisting that Death surrender. Pitted obelisks poke like
empty cannons firing at the sky; juniper shoots its bright blue
balls against oblivion.

For every weapon, there are leaning willows, swags of laurel,
sheaves of wheat. Slim stone virgins whisper comfort. Broad
stone bosoms welcome weeping, lilies, forgetfulness.

From the fragile Piaf to the firm Molière, from the fragile
Chopin to the firm Colette. Heloise and Abelard. Oscar
Wilde. Sarah Bernhardt. Simone de Beauvoir. Lives charred
with meaning.

The bodies through which work comes become at death a place
to go to offer thanks, to leave a blossom, to pat the old stone
shoulders of the ancestors.

A little wisteria-bound building houses a toilet that's only a hole
in the tile floor. Two feet on the platform. Step out of the way of
the dowsing flush. Pee, don't rest, say the ghosts. Get on with
life. Much to be done before you finish.

Wander, winding through pines and impermanence. The
silence is quieted by the soft tap of chisel on stone. New
names to add.

Beaucoup De Gens

Touring the Tour Eiffel was too challenging to be a pleasure. You long to open—to the sky, to the city, to the great tradition— but everything conspires to cramp you, make you defensive. Crush of crowds, people press behind and front. A living tower of Babylon for all the languages spoken. The crushing smell of many unbathed people. People cutting in front of us to the elevator we had patiently waited for. Knee-buckling ride up to the levels. Let me off, let me off, though I married a man who likes to go to the top of everything. I cannot leave him to marvel by himself.

From the very top we see crowds below, the hatted folk we thought at first were Muslim, but then realized they were Americans in baseball caps. They have gathered, not terribly well, into three rows spelling:

JENUN

PARIS

The "Ns" (meant to be "Ss") had a particularly difficult time arranging themselves.

We walked down. The fresh air did me good.

I prefer The Eiffel Tower we met on our first jet-lagged day.

◇◇◇

A mother dips her baby's feet into a fountain. Lovers, as expected, everywhere—wrapped in creative embraces. Kisses flash like sunlight off the Seine. A tall tough wears a Trojan waving from his backpocket. An older woman, hair the shade of a new flowerpot, in a frilly suit cut down to here and up to there totters at a payphone, calling up her youth on four inch strappy heels.

Women elegant with self-assurance, black sweaters tossed simply over their shoulders, like Jackie. Women who pluck and polish, but don't primp; who wear loosely knotted scarves and carry good bags and baguettes. Others structure themselves in boxes of bouclé hinged with massive necklaces.

◊◊◊

We return to the Louvre to peer into the shadowed corners of Vermeer. After partaking of the absolute satisfaction of his ordered world, we emerge from the glass pyramid into flocks of people ambling toward the Tuileries, as if someone had gently tipped the Plaza. We know where they are headed and we are ambivalent.

Today the great Lance Armstrong will bag his third Tour de France win. (In the years before his scandal, we all regarded him as a tremendous athlete and an inspiring person.) Here we are, in Paris, not far from the finish line. The Tour de France will conclude, as always, with several rounds of cycling down the Champs-Élysées. But we had seen part of the Champs-Élysées a few days earlier and it was one of our few disappointments—a wide, beautifully planted avenue plastered with gauche touristy shops.

The Triomphe here is American culture, and it is not a pretty sight after the authenticity of the streets we had been walking. We turned off it after a few blocks because it took us so far away from Paris. Did we really want to join surging crowds straining for a view in this disheartening neighborhood? Why go except to brush with greatness, to see a legend in the flesh, to breathe the air he stirs?

Wanting to go and rather not-ing. Let's leave the crowds to themselves and read about it on the plane tomorrow. Then we spot a cluster of people gathered on the Plaza. We walk over.

There is a low concrete wall, and as we arrive, two people leave. We lean over the wall and look down.

We are standing on a roadway overpass. One second later, a police car zooms through. Three or four more cars—team cars! A perfect unobstructed view. A whir as of wings and speeding cyclists spurt beneath our feet. From this angle the working rounded backs in brilliant jerseys look like so many colored bubbles—a rolling boil of effort. Among them, sharp and clear, streaks an acid flash of sulfur yellow. "Lance!" we cheer and clap along with everyone. It is over in a second—the comet and his attendant meteors vanish instantly. Our blood is carbonated by the thrill of witness. A bright yellow package slips into memory: a great man in a great moment.

Pilgrimage

We make a pilgrimage to 27 rue de Fleurus, where Gertrude and Alice and their merry band thought up twentieth-century art and letters. The building, of toasted grey stone, is powerful and formal in the Stein way. Above the door, a noble carved Romanesque head observes the comings and goings, expressing perfectly her spirit. From the street we see through ample windows the ceilings of the second floor stamped with the voices, the arguments, the passions of Picasso, Matisse, Rousseau, Hemingway, Fitzgerald, countless lesser luminaries.

We think of that birth of Art and the birth of the War and the Occupation and find, for all its charm and luxury, there is no way to be in Paris and not reflect on struggle. It is a

place on the faultline of social struggle, as likely to have
revolutions in thought in art and letters and politics as
California has earthquakes. All around the city vast gold-
leafed commemorations of heroism, military triumph,
plaques commemorating people caught in spattering
gunfire, Resistance fighters. It is no surprise the Resistance
triumphed—given the strong ideas of what life should be here.

Napoleon. Liberté, Égalité, Fraternité inscribed. Broken noses,
mutilated statues, the fury of the people, the golden Joan of
Arc, that simple peasant girl mightily enshrined in gold astride
her steed. Names hacked off the streets. Home of the mob. The
Bastille. The grand Army that poured through the streets, the
defense of French soil. Artists manning bandages, people of
practical heart. Their way of life makes it understandable why
they worked so hard to preserve it.

Very little Paris is pretend.

Les Boutiques

Quiet little man in the lampshade shop overlooking a tiny
square. Silky glow of orange, green, yellow lampshades, well-
cut silhouettes in iron dancing, farming, skiing with pleated
shades like military decorations. Serene Chinoiserie, hand-
painted plumy birds. Tight calicos of blossom. Workroom right
in the next room, see him stretch silk over the wire frame,
dousing it with tassels.

Oil shop ten feet wide. You know without tasting that the
quality must be excellent—the rent on the Rue Saint-Jacob
is astronomical.

The bouquinistes: a holy, inherited profession. Green wooden box-shops full of etchings, old art, yellowed books, but newly brave, too—avant-garde film, political screeds, fancy advertising art, sway in the breeze. The past seasoned with the future. Closed, the shops are like books you cannot open.

Île Saint-Louis, sheltered, quiet and windy, like a tiny pantry to Paris. Windows full of shining jars of jams and relish, toys and the densest most flavorful ice cream—deep chocolate and cherry.

A brilliant chocolate shop of Aztec inspiration: bright summery colors turquoise and marigold, chocolate hunks and bricks and chunks and tiles, decorated tiles of chocolate as if around an ancient Aztec fountain. Little Quetzalcoatls, jaguars, headdressed birds delicately painted dark and sweet. We buy an inch-thick slab of nut bark, best we ever ate, rocky with pistachios, almonds, hazelnuts.

A guidebook recommends a Parisian department store for knobs—a fantasy of hardware as if concocted at the patisserie: flowers, leaves, mammals, bugs, every geometry, sober and whimsical, knobs, hinges, pulls in metal, plastic, wood, resin. Six golden swags of laurel ornament this desk at which I write.

Autres Plaisirs

The marvelous button shop, the wit of hats, the great gilded ornate well of Les Galeries Lafayette, the symphonic elegance of Luxembourg Gardens. Lampshades and fixtures like whimsical pastries. Confectionary architecture.

The organ grinder with a dog and cat asleep together in a little bed next to him.

The perfect behavior of French dogs, even in the most elegant of restaurants. Manners.

Long red coat in the window, stunning cascade of bouclé.

The shiny green enamel muse fountains on the street. The swaggering Metro entrances. Little ornamental carousels.

The breakfast bread. The terrific pillows. Soap and paper in every toilette. Any café is good for hot chocolate. Objects and the tremendous sky—wide, unsullied, ornamented with the nineteenth century—great Ferris wheels and La Tour Eiffel.

Fine old French faces. Powerful sensitive noses appraising, appreciating. Features repeated since the Bayeux tapestry, alive here delivering, driving, conducting.

People brought up with certainty about how life is lived. Because *this* is how it is done. How food is cooked and served. How linens are pressed. How sex, art, music, light, space, and greenery are necessary to life. How life is meant to be a pleasure. City of the senses. To a certain extent this is true of any city, but in Paris the refinement is secure and ancient.

Paris lives as dream and aspiration: frilly and stony, gritty and smooth, old as hope, fresh as lettuce, opulent as vaulted gold and simple as bread.

One of life's great privileges is to share Paris with the love of your life, and for this I thank the marvelous man I married.

Not many things have this romantic genuine ancient & authentic a basis.

It's enough just to say

Paris.

Art supplies.

Technologies

Tapdance

The title above prompted this reflection when I heard my husband laugh. The scrap of paper I'd scribbled it on had fallen from my pocket and he picked it up, puzzled and amused. It's the locomotive and the caboose of a train of thought that runs this way:

It's an outright miracle that when we have questions nowadays, we have access to a beautiful instant mass of answers. I'm not even talking fumbling in fusty cubicles with microfilm and microfiche. Questions that might have occasioned a phonecall some years ago now only warrant not even a push of a button, but a simple tap for an answer.

Not a tap like one hammered into a maple tree, and the subsequent patient weeks as the pail fills. Not a tap born of years of sweaty practice that result in a crackling-clickety-rhythmic Ruby Keeler number. Not even the effort it takes to pull a mug of draft beer. Answers appear with the softest of taps: fingertip on screen.

Everything's on tap now—music, movies, books, pictures, communication, friends themselves, it seems. Hot and cold running information, entertainment, communication available round the clock at our slightest whim. The genie seeps out with less effort than it takes to rub a lamp.

It means many answers no longer have to be violently wrested from life. But this also means that I might not call my piecrust friend for advice on finessing a bushel of peaches. Why "bother" her when I can get the answer online without disturbing her day?

Of course, the genie won't fill you in on the first tooth or the polished manuscript or the quirky cousin. The genie can't pick up your child, pour you refreshment when you're tapped out, or make you ache with uproarious laughter. The genie won't ask you for any favors, but it can't do you any, either. And it can't volunteer your time, either.

With all due respect to the genie, many of life's most meaningful answers arrive only in physical action and interaction. As we tap, tap, tap, let's remember to tap the many delights of three-dimensional friendship. Take an action. Call a friend. Volunteer. Remember, even websites themselves exist because people take action.

Too much anything

is good for nothing.

Derailed and Rerailed

Last week, a derailment occurred on Metro North, the commuter train that I and thousands take in and out of Manhattan. Happily, there were no injuries—it was ten cars full of garbage—but it happened at the very narrowest, rockiest section of the railroad, blocking passage for three days. Yet by Monday, everything was back to normal.

How on earth did they do it? You can see in a video *The New York Times* called "surprisingly fascinating." I'll share with you what interested me.

Using a huge crane, they lift a big freight box off a derailed car and settle it onto another car on the parallel track. It was almost like the old "15" puzzle, with only one small useable space.

What was most revelatory to me was how they made that useable space. They dismantled a section of tracks! Seeing the rails and crossties all undone amazed me. Why? Because the railroad seems permanent. Not unlike certain systems of belief, which take our minds from place to place.

Even though we forget, both are made of components which can be disassembled when we get derailed. When our trains of thought are not smoothly conveying us where we want to go, we can jump the rails, or even reroute our whole journey.

It's also grand to see how people of clever vision working together can accomplish what looks impassible and impossible.

Angle Matters

You know her, but do you know her from this angle? Fine-boned, luminous, pearly-white, she rises from the vivid green in the company of well-proportioned alabaster relatives.

From this angle, we enter and climb this narrowstepped, carefully-restored marble privilege. Feel the tower's kinesthetic truth in the angle of our ankles, our limbs teetering out, then in, our tilting spines spiraling up the dim cramped stairway like passing through the tight and curling body of a dark seashell until we dizzily emerge into the blinding blue air at the top.

From this angle, terracotta roofs lead the eye like flagstones to the brushy olive hills and the iris-blue Apennines. Who knew she was so beautifully sited?

There's a definite jolt of pleasure in seeing a famous landmark (or a person) from the angle you expect. Even if a pizza box trained you.

But we live in a world of three dimensions, a world of innumerable angles.

Let's look around, above, beneath, behind the flat screens in our hands and our minds. Let's play with a few acute and obtuse angles before we declare the "right" angle. Sometimes the rightest angle is several degrees from plumb. So the Tower of Pisa teaches.

Words on a Page

Waiting for a train I heard one young woman tell another, "My brother says, 'Why should I read? It's just words on a page.' "

Struck me to the heart, these words in the air. And though I'm selling tuxedos to penguins, should someone ever ask you...

"Why board a train?" I want to say. "It's just cars on a track. It only gets you places hard to get to on your own and a whole lot faster."

But shock occasions reflection and reflection, gratitude.

Words on a page. Important, like boxcars, for what they convey. Which is us.

Reading, we ride with the engineer. Worlds of our joint creation spring up around the locomotive.

Nonfiction writers can take us anywhere—this author explored the Arctic, for example, so I can share somewhat in that experience. What expert scouts good writers are!

Fiction writers take us inside each other, inside ourselves. They train our inner ear to our inner life—that slippery ongoing stream of psychological states which filter, flow and congeal into physical experience.

And poets? Well, they don't use tracks at all. They just beam us from place to place.

Isn't it wonderful, this magical travel through each other's minds and experiences? Even if sometimes the page is glowing glass, not paper.

Stream your consciousness.

Phorgotten Phone

Flying out West to visit family, I phound I'd phorgotten my phone. Turned out my brother forgot his, too. We laughed and guessed we did not want to be distracted during this eight-day family trip.

Fast-backward to the early eighties. Every youthful explorer of consciousness has a whopping enlightenment experience or two. Mine came in '81 and lasted several months. During this acceleration, my artist friends, the streets of New York, domestic life—everything—was intense, colorful, deeply meaningful and I wanted to record it all.

I carried a notebook and pen for words, a clipboard and brushpen for on-the-spot sketching, a heavy-lensed camera, a hand-sized tape recorder for musical inspirations and conversations, plus fresh batteries, film and extra cassettes. In the days before cargo pants. I was a veritable communications packhorse. It was thrilling to have such capacities, albeit cumbersome.

When smartphones appeared, I recognized that all I had sought was now in a single trim item, with Dick Tracy's two-way wrist-radio and a video camera thrown in. Plus you can read a book, answer most questions and talk with the people you love.

So, eight days with no phone. What did I miss? Other people could place and take my calls for the duration and I so rarely text that that was no inconvenience. I had another way to check email, and though I sometimes capture a floating melody, I don't record conversations anymore, or do many al fresco drawings. And I still carry a notebook rather than typing my observations.

But I missed that camera. I know the faces of my family, and I'm continually drawn to the same behaviors of light. But life, while mellowed, is still intense, colorful and deeply meaningful. Happily, though, some images can be shared in words.

Tapping Power

Last week a yellow waterlily opened up a world.

I went to California to visit my sister Kako in her excellent Memory Care Unit. Spending time with an Alzheimer's patient will challenge your habits. The two pillars of ordinary conversation—what has been and what is coming—are essentially meaningless.

Of course, it's our cultural expectations that are limited, not the person. So much capacity remains: to experience, to feel, to laugh, to enjoy the familiar. But side by side in the present you must remain. What can we share?

As we smiled together over lunch, I remembered I had some family pictures on my iPad, so I pulled it out. Kako loved the familiar nameless faces and enjoyed looking at my landscape and flower photos.

Then I opened my wonderful Poetry app and read her some funny old rhythm and rhyme pieces—James Whitcomb Riley, Edward Lear. She was especially delighted with "Casey at the Bat."

As I went from photo to photo and app to app, I swung the iPad away from her, concerned that the zaps and zooms might disturb her.

But when I opened up Monet and gently slid from painting to painting, she reached out and double-tapped that yellow waterlily. It of course instantly enlarged, which tickled her. She tapped the blossom in and out and soon discovered that she could change the pictures herself with a slide of her finger.

"Would you like to make some art of your own?" I opened up a sketching app and we made some abstract pictures together. After that, a beautiful meditative Japanese game. She loved making the little explorer move back and forth in his peaceful luminous world.

"I like this," she said. "It takes me out of myself."

By the time I left, we had spent three hours together, the longest visit we have had in many years, all because we'd found a way into her almost vanished world of volition. The staff was happy to hear it and will now assist her with an iPad every day, taking her out of herself and into her power.

Technology itself is not the answer. Presence is. But I do offer gratitude for this varied, entertaining means of sharing it.

Once you know the ropes,

show them.

Fragilities

The Cookie Crumbles

Memory

"My first memory of kindergarten," I say to my older sister, "is sweeping out the playhouse. And the nap. And snack."

Yawning waitress sets down steamy mugs of tea. "Cookies'll be right out."

"I don't remember kindergarten," sighs my sister. Nor today's trip to the Memory Clinic, or the tissue-stuffed purse in her hand. "Would you have a Kleenex?"

Memories of theatre training: Listen to your partner. However many repetitions, create the Illusion of The First Time. Remember your objective.

Which is what?

1. To remember her memories for her?

Pluck a Kleenex from her bag. Hand it to her.

"Here you go." Her embarrassed laugh.

"I bet you remember other things from childhood."

Wrinkles of uncertainty. Then:

"Mother played piano to calm us in the war."

"Really? I never knew she played. What songs?"

Audible thud of doubt.

Buzz of customers. Beeping ditty of the register. Waitress groans under a tray.

2. If I don't save her memory of Mother at the spinet in apron and up-do, diverting her youngsters in '43, is a nugget of truth gone for good?

Then a fragile smile. Her shyly reedy voice: "Mairzy doats and dozey doats and little lambsy divey. A kiddley divey too, wouldn't you?"

I laugh, softly join her.

Memory's longest resident: melody. This I remember, clear as clove, from Mom's decline.

3. If I collect her memories, do they displace mine cooling on the rack?

Yet like yeast, our memories multiply. Already: me remembering her remembering Mom remembering Mairzy Doats. Like the repartee of multiplied reflections in the mirrors in the black-and-peach-tiled eighth floor ladies' room where Mom took us after tea and shortbread after shopping: us washing us washing us again washing. Infinite uses in infinite spaces.

"Here you go, ladies. Ginger for you—"

"Nope, she gets chocolate chip."

Is forgetfulness contagious?

"Sorry. Daughters kept me up." She rotates the plates. "More tea water?'

"We're good." Off she shuffles.

"Oh goody! We never get cookies."

Except every day at her residence.

"I'll ask the staff to put them on the menu."

"I'll bake you a batch tomorrow when I get back to Los Angeles," she says. "I'm really looking forward to going home. I'm taking the train since I sold my car."

4. Is memory truth?

Nutmegs of truth, webbed in mace of fancy.

Truth

5. Truth is?

Any body next to us, for one thing. Especially if we grew up with her. If she and her poodle skirt and her despair influenced us. Family is truth's kindergarten.

"I don't remember kindergarten."

I don't remember my objective. To understand truth?

Yet at the Memory Clinic, she remembered:

"I've been diagnosed with Alzheimer's."

No hesitation in this truth. No faltering.

Balder than truth. Nonfiction. Nonfiction blasts forth. Gets on with it. Every couple minutes to the social worker: "I've been diagnosed with Alzheimer's. Would you have a Kleenex?"

Truth is a byproduct of nonfiction.

Nonfiction

6. Are questions always nonfiction?

7. Are our lives nonfiction because they are one long question?

Nonfiction has no time to speculate.

Fiction we worship from childhood: characters, yearning, sweet plotisfaction. *At the end she wakes up. At the end there's a cure. At the end from the rafters: Kleenex ex Machina.*

Fiction receives the tiara. Nonfiction, her mother, is sweeping and swearing and paying the bills. An embarrassed laugh.

Nonfiction is snapping the plastic bag in the bin for the daughters she'll need to feed and divert tonight. Boyfriends and braces and night class. Divorce, which is always nonfiction. Disease.

Which makes my sister wince at shocking pink, at china mugs chucked in the bus tub. Infuriates her with a toddler's squeal. "How can they bring children here!" Which shakes her with sobbing delusion. This bright sweet frustration whose life I can't save, whose past I can't store. Nonfiction crashes like a tank over students.

Nonfiction is the name of every urgency.

Nonfiction gets drunk sings farts fucks stabs. Bears it all: madness, adultery, tedium, chemo. But it's the elbow as well as the knife in the rib. The belly laugh. An arm and a stick and a picket fence. A wad of gum and a bucket of rubies. Coffee and sleep and mysterious, sensible dream.

Galaxy-wide, multiplied.

Nonfiction is revolution, when it cannot stand it anymore. Nonfiction lodges every dagger of the human heart, each arrow of the gods. Ninety tornadoes cluster through the south, smashing also mansions. Families are huddling each other even now.

Nonfiction is need.

Fiction is yearning.

Truth is reflection.

Memory's moot.

She needs none of these.

She's eaten her cookie. She'd like a Kleenex.

What to Tell and When

He's my oldest friend. She is his last living relative. They call each other "Brother" and "Sister."

She's watching him open a birthday present. If she hadn't insisted on a party and traveled to New York last week, Brother might have let the milestone slip.

Sister has a longer journey up ahead. Medication is no longer working. When she leaves depends on what is dissolving and what is resolving within her. But it is near enough that tonight I'm prompted to ask, "What do you want him to know when you're gone? What can I tell him you said?"

"Oh so much, so much. I'd have to sit and write it down."

"And so you might, but what's the first thing that popped into your head?"

"Admiration. I want him to know I admire him, how much he's been through, all the obstacles he's overcome." We share a rich and satisfying conversation that helps me know my old friend even better, words which will help me help him when he needs it.

The lighted cake appears, the song is sung, cards and gifts are opened and it's time for us to go. I take Brother aside to say good night. Suddenly, I think, *Why wait till she's gone?* We can't know love too soon or too often.

"I'm going to tell you something tonight, and then I'm gonna tell you again another time." I told him what I'd asked and what she said. I'll tell him again when the time comes.

If someone you know will be leaving us, perhaps you can offer such an opportunity. Love, expressed in the present, put by for the future, when this is the past. No wonder they say it's eternal.

Even love

needs love.

An Argument with Water

Journey's end, our final blue Aegean day. Shockingly, you book a swim trip. You hate swimming. A pool's for cooling ankles, a shiverdip on triple-digit days. You carry from another life an argument with water, an argument unsettled by your swimming-teacher father.

Did you forget it? Let it go? Or did you test it, that brilliant sea-smashed morning boarding the tidy charter?

A dozen tawny bodies unfolding on the deck. Young entwining hands, unlike ours, ringless. A friendly bunch. Gentle laughter, quiet marvels. Swelling sails, whitecaps, gem-blue waves. Soon, an oxblood promontory. Smiles. Yours, too. Fricative shutterclicks.

Fathoms evaporate. Red rock yields to chalkwhite stone. We anchor. I have arguments, but none with water. Off the stern I slip. Under glaciery crumbling towers, I frolic in the cove; you snap shots from the deck. On we sail. Limerock yields to runnelled pumice, pitchblack beach. Another anchoring.

Is the answer in the fine professor's lecture months ago: "Swim, swim the hotsprings if you can?" What made you leap your ancient lapping fear, slide into this second bay, tread water next to me, whisper as we clamber up, "I'll stay in longer, next time?" Next time, why did doubt leap with you?

Third anchor-drop.

We ladder to the water, push off, aiming for the golden cove: balmy hot springs maybe twenty boat-lengths off—aiming to relax, but suddenly swells   churned by swimmer-loaded boats—everyone's longing to float, to relax—

saltwater spasms toss us,
            lurch us,   keeping our heads

above water   now a living idiom. I swim on, glance
                  for you over my bobbing shoulder.

     "I' m not
          do ing
              so   well,"
      you
               gasp.   I plunge to you,

hold you. *It's fine. We'll swim to that rock*

    —miraculous skinny upright poking up just where we need
it, miraculous chain looped over it—
        Grab   this,   I'll swim back for lifejackets.
               Breathe.   We'll be fine.

Did I doubt for a moment your strength, your survival? Never.
You'd never die now, on the brink of such wonder. But I felt
your doubt and your fear, for you swim and surf in emotion,
fearlessly challenge its swells.

Hold on, I'll be back with a lifejacket.

I don't want to leave you alone with your fear.

Instead, we conjure up—miraculous—a young man brisking
through the surges.

"Can I bring you some life jackets?"

"Yes!" Later, on deck, we note on his shoulders: scars, peculiar
as wing-stubs.

We talk about it, as we always talk. You insist you called to me for help. "Not aloud," I said. "But that's why I glanced when I did." After years of listening, silent and aloud are one.

You like to say I saved your life. I maintain no life is saved against its will, and if I heard you call me inwardly, I also heard you tell me not to worry. After all, you had breath to speak.

Why did you book a swim trip? You can say it was for me, or hotsprings, but you dove into your argument with water, headlong into courage, fear and rescue. Through emotion you are not afraid to swim. Where your broken father had his argument.

Where full fathom five, he lies.

Geographies

City of Strings

Always a violin playing somewhere in this somber glowing city, two cities, once, Buda and Pest, two truths knit, city of strings.

While America yellows like old plastic, Europe crumbles like desiccated stucco. In once-graceful avenues of Budapest, embellishment like crusted frosting brittles and shatters; graffiti knifes her grand facades: typical obscenities and the plaintive, "Have a good day before your life is gone."

Many-booted city, many meats. Young women, loose and leathered, flash bright smiles, suck red chicken legs. Trim old women in toques of twisted felt, scrutinize the butchershop: selection, inspection, string-wound purchase, ruled precisely as a cardgame. Café cardgame, five old men, Cezanne sprung to life—how many years have they met, how many times a week— crumpled old friends, fraying their moustaches, twisting their cigarettes, nipping noon brandies and ham. Rain drove the sidewalk café through the door, stacks of battered folded chairs and tables shift like cards in gnarled hands, slide, collapse. Young men leap the heap coming in for sausages. No one, not even the tough stringy waiter, moves to pick them up.

Here and there, though, sumptuous revival. Lapsed in the '40s to an exquisite warehouse, the historic New York Café—scene of literary, artistic, cinematic foment—is now restored to glory. Sonic in gilded intensity, pillars, pilasters, pastries of glittering ornament, pastilles and baskets of gold leaf, ceiling murals like platters of meat and fish amid the nymphs and demons of dessert. Wrought iron balustrades undulating into cornucopias, the floor a massive layered slab of marble torte.

This chorus of glorious ornament, once just for altars, once just for God, and what did God become? Hoops of writers, artists, round these tables, debating, creating, testing ideas, revolutions, fueled by liver and goosefat and paprikash, pickles and coffee and whipping cream wheeled up on brass-handled trolleys. This hall, and all the temples of theatre, opera, art, music here in the city of strings echoed with the voice of God in human timbre.

Now this chorus of ornament only for commerce? Just a spectacular shell for the hermit crab tourists? This, but not just.

Here, elbows on a scalloped chocolate tablecloth, blonde skein barely clasped, blushy cheek, pale plum mouth, a living painting of a woman leans, dimpled fingers feeding éclair to her scruffy lover.

Here, bending and retrieving fried potatoes underneath the high chair, catching a mittenstring over his ear, a patient bag-eyed mousehaired papa makes a baby laugh.

Here, toasting, clinking, sipping, a dozen matrons celebrating their museum. Thanks to them, the art the painters argued over is preserved and viewed, the books the writers wept about are read and circulated. Ornament for passion, for family, ornament again for art.

Older still, the healing waters. Ancient Turkish baths, starry domes. Heat and pummeling. Echoing laughter and lovers entwined with the world on a string. Certainly sweat and repose. Certainly. Certainly songs and liquors and arms around shoulders. Yet rancor threads through the worn dressing gown of this town.

Angry young spray their strings of invective. The older women, the twisted felts, bear their blasted youth like unborn children.

Stones formed in their wombs when rolling grey boulders of
soldiers crushed fathers, felled brothers, pulped their virginity.
Their bodies stiffened, never to release, spirits still in spasm.
The husbands in this country shove its rate of suicide nearly to
the highest in the world, a special code in their obituaries: "The
sudden and tragic death of..."

Take this iron face above her string of jade, below her cloche
of moss. These fingers hooking the string of the bakery box
loosened, perhaps, a noose. Her steely eye, her set mouth tells
nothing. Secure in the box, meringue piled on pudding on jam-
slathered cakes, sweets upon sweets. Nothing is sweet enough.

Later she'll attend the string quartet, nursery of tears.

Mongol, Ottoman, Nazi, Communist—grief too old and too
recent weaves through burnt velvet streets, tangles the warp
and woof, knots in the eyelets of shoes.

Sixty pair in cast iron strung along the riverbank, stone's throw
from Parliament: 1940s boots, heels, galoshes, baby shoes.
Inside them, burning candles, shriveled berries, tiny apples,
bits of ribbon, commemorate barefoot Jews shot into the stone-
shouldered Danube, drowning, as their warm and precious
shoes were stuffed into soldiers' rucksacks. Bodies rolling on
blood-thickened currents, some gathered downriver in nets of
stained string.

The shooters' fury birthed, perhaps, when World War I
strung up this country like a thrashing doe and let the dogs
have at her.

A triple million kindred slain, left of her ten largest cities just
two, left of her lands but 30 percent; all her gold, her silver,
copper, stolen: plundered her timber, her seaports, her banks.
And if your body were this country, with both legs and an

arm torn away, your bowels devoured, three-fourths of your face erased?

World War II left you half-dead; Communism, hanging by a thread.

Still, twist strengthens string. Bow strings, to launch arrows, must be tight. Even beads need knots.

Budapest's a destination now. In both her moods: Grand hotels and the House of Terror. Sleek cars and yarnsmocked blouses. Sightseeing boats and worn-out shoes.

Strings of notes, songs on plucked strings and strummed strings seep over music school sills, notes caramelized in French horn spill into the streets.

Steps of tiles up steep roofs, overlapping patterns, green and yellow, intricate and lepidopteral, scaly eyebrow windows raised at the copper spires, barbed towers, catscradle skyline. Bending silver branches weeping at the synagogue. Bombed church repacified in grass. Liszt bronzed in his colossal torque of passion. Vest-pocket puppetshop, pirates and princesses, whimsy and villainy dangle on strings. Old women tilt their hats, barkeeps pour palinka, plasterers mount scaffolding. In dark workshops fragrant with maplewood, catgut is stretched over ebony fingerboards, pulled into tension.

Pain

is the ghost

that haunts us all.

Walking South

What can one body do?

They do not want my blood. I gave them money, Advil and Excedrin, the tent in our garage, a batch of cookies. What else can I give? What else?

Eyes. Words.

It's Saturday. My oldest friend, who has not left the '70s since Tuesday, meets me at Grand Central. Together we'll walk south.

I have no TV. Late Tuesday night, we visited some friends. We saw the crash and topple on their set, but by choice, I've missed the blast of images that blew across the world this week. I see it all for the first time in person.

One.

Out of Grand Central. Flyers hook our eyes. *MISSING HELP US FIND.* Faces, torn off the refrigerator, scanned in panic; mostly young and smiling. *A cast from toe to knee. A silver tooth. A hip replaced.*

Curious details. Personal. Charms, scars, badges of life.

When I grasp they are identifying marks to certify what is unbearable, my veins run ice and acid.

107th floor PLEASE HELP. Brother, sister worked together. Windows on the World. Whale and dolphin circling a starfish tattooed on his right arm.

Two.

Down Lexington. Flyers, faces, multiply until they touch,
shoulder over shoulder, at the Armory. The Wall of Hope:
a haunted yearbook taped to brick. Faces, flowers. *Any
information please expecting his first child.*

"Please step to the other side of the street so we can get
through. Thank you."

People wheeling shopping carts of sandwiches; people holding
clipboards answer questions; people stunned.

Red tent for the media, to share with other worlds what limbo's
like, Hell's border, souls' transition.

"DNA Testing Office" scrawled on cardboard. I ask my friend.
His answer socks my gut. Loved ones bring in dirty underwear,
toothbrushes of the missing, hoping one of the million body
parts will match the DNA. Confirmation intimate, ultimate.

"Please step to the other side of the street so we can get
through. Thank you."

Three.

Crossing the avenues. Could you see them from here? I don't
remember. Oh, but from here, my god the steam, the smoke,
the smolder. Still.

Stop for omelets. Lozenge of time to rest, to sip, to talk
prosaically, to see if we remember how to laugh. We smile at
Chelsea style and a vest-pocket Lhasa Apso puppy; then limp
back to our work: observation.

Four.

Stunned swarms circle Union Square; in debate, in whimpers,
in silence asking is this anything like anything we've ever
known, knowing it is not. Inside out, our flesh: heart, shock,
hope hate fear exposed in this broad biopsy of trauma.

The air above these thousands of bewildered heads is too
critical to disturb with painted wishes; banners drape the steps.
*End the Desperation That Leads to Terrorism. An Eye for an
Eye Makes Two Blind People.* One wordless banner, laid like
altarcloth: simple, light-specked bright concentric rainbow.

Prayer stalls hand out pamphlets, food and water. A halo many
people deep begins *Amazing Grace.*

Concrete softens with the candleshrines. Sabbath tapers
next to Spanish blessing candles, votives set on kente cloth.
Faiths mingling like petals, ribbons. Waxes blending, heavy
multicolored tears congealing on the ground.

People wander, wonder what they need, and find it is to gather,
weep, to speak, to sing, to ask, to be in open air, to search each
other's face, to give comfort and to seek it. We need to feel the
charge across our skins, the knowledge of one body.

Five.

A few silent blocks. Washington Square. Canvas panels stretch
across a cyclone fence erected round the arch; cups of felt-tip
markers at the ready. A place for the hand to respond: to write,
to draw, to join the prayers and curses, pictures, vulgar and
evolved. Take it all, venom with the sweet, obscene with sacred.

Outpouring into each other, pain, lives, money, emotion. Hemorrhaging into each other all that moves in our one body.

I commit my heart to peace in all forms and offer gratitude to those who sacrificed and suffered for my awareness. I sign. My friend draws the towers with pride and love.

We cannot tarry to hear the guitarist, or watch as people fill the canvas. I have a train to catch, home to reach, but first, as south as we can get.

Six.

Dozens of bulldozers lining the streets near Canal. Cavalry, ready when needed. Ahead, the blockade. Canal's as far as we can go.

White smoke and steam plume up behind police like thought or soul or tears evaporating, or distillation of a memory of nephews on the observation deck, or the slipstream of the celebration of our marriage license: lunch at Windows on The World.

These ether off like life.

Swing of a microphone under a tent, camera lights flash on a man and a woman, exhausted, knocking off rockdust from hard hats, fluorescent vests. It dawns on my shock-thickened brain. *They've been doing The Work.*

They're worn out from pulling at rubble, they long for a bath and a meal and a bed, but first they want to speak. I cannot hear, but I can see them growing strong before the camera. Neither they nor the earnest reporter can tell it's not the camera lights that nourish them but their own surprise at what they did. They were as helpful as instinct, and only their cells recognize it. All of the cells of this one body know, as the cells of this one body answer this wound.

Seven.

Bookstore. Grand Central. Page through a commonplace NYC calendar. Its sweet confidence, and its bold glitzy shots are history. Our souvenirs have turned to artifacts.

Skyline of New York, beloved, personal, as the roof line of the house I own.

Chimney knocked off now. Burning furnace of finance backed up, choking on its smoke without the customary upward draw.

Eight.

How will we remember that day? A day we went from consumers to citizens.

A day we understood the grief and fear in other countries. A day our country left its adolescence. A day we knew we could die. A day life became precious. A day we grew up. A day we knew as one body our pain. As one body our fear. As one body our tears. As one body our bravery. As one body our anger. As one body our hope. As one body a city tall and a world wide. One body, even with those who hurt us.

Prayers, curses, venom, sweet, havoc, health, take it all. Our heart beats loud and fast, the better to hear it.

Life was practice up till then, or school. This incendiary graduation with its haunted yearbook threw us sink or swimming into selves we thought ourselves incapable of being.

We're not made of matter

but of mattering.

Tell of Israel

In archeology, a tell is an artificial hill created by many generations of people living and rebuilding on the same spot. Over time, the level rises, forming a mound.

Time As Tell

Night begins the day, we learn the night we arrive. For Jews and Muslims both, the night belongs to the day that follows it. After sundown, when the first three stars appear, the new day begins. Our day one begun.

From Tel Aviv our host drives us through the light-pricked dark of the West Bank. *Green means mosque*, she tells us. Late we reach her home above the Sea of Galilee, fall into the dreamless.

Morning and a visit to a diplomat, whose farmer husband tells us *95 percent of people here have lost a loved one. 95 percent. I: my brother. Young.*

We journey and he points. *Ancient Roman site.* He tells stories of Josephus. And his own: *I rescued someone from this river once. Next time I came, I heard a guide describe the rescue to his group, stating **he** had done it. The guides tell lies to fascinate their clients.*

Our trip accelerates. We are guests, we have no say.

Fighter planes in tight formation, crisp as dress uniforms. Scratchy broadcast call to prayer. *The border is right there. That's the border.* Triple border: Syria. Jordan. Israel. Peacekeepers. Thudding artillery.

River Jordan. Temple to Pan. Ceasarea Maritima. Herod's palace. *In this corner, Paul was two years imprisoned.*

Tel Megiddo

You cannot dig here but you find.

Dig. Noun and verb. Head archeologist tells: *We no longer scrape off whole layers. Now just a square, just a trench at a time, leaving much untouched for future, better methods.*

Layers of life merge incrementally, until the eye opens into the Early Bronze Age: a perfect moon of basalt, five thousand years old. Part of a massive temple it may take five thousand meticulous years to reveal.

Time Will Tell

This was just discovered. This was a hip of dirt piled to that ledge till nineteen sixty-seven. This is the border.

Skeletal synagogue, patches of fresco, carved menorah stone, tripod feet, flaming wheels. Carved and painted, grown and eaten, precious yet today—the seven species of antiquity: fig pomegranate date grape olive wheat barley.

Journey As Tell

Facts stories events introductions privileges days nights meals pile on each other.

No time to excavate. We are guests. We have no say. Move on. Experience mounds on experience. Sunset. Three stars. New day.

Tell Stories

This journalist, a light in his eyes like a lamp passing behind an iron door. He confesses, *Poetry is my deepest heart but I do not tell it. My world is not friendly to poets, to readers of poems; readers of poems become poets, poets read feelings, respond to the world. The world is not kind. I cover news.* His eyes darken. The iron door shuts.

This kibbutznik musician tells his communal upbringing left him free to roam the fields but not to see his parents, at work for the common good. His wife stuffs crumpled spears of lemongrass into a battered pot, serves the quenching tea with crunchy peanuts big as knuckles. Shows us then her studio, her brawny terracotta sculptures.

They met here at the kibbutz bomb shelter. Bomb shelter. *Every house has one.* Paper plates, household junk on the bunks.

The day we are to tour the secret bullet factory, I decline and pace instead the planted courtyard in bird-embellished silence.

This museum director tells, *Intifada, from the Arabic: tremor, shivering, shuddering. Bursts of terror. Can you take a bus becomes the question. "If your bus blows up, Son, make them bring you here to this emergency room. Your brother's having his cast replaced."*

One day I came home. Long-range weapons had damaged my house and my neighbors'.

"That's it," they said. "We're leaving."

Soberly we nod in her garden reclaimed, among her olives, bay, roses. Garlic big as baby fists twists over her table.

Next day, when they returned—

"Your neighbors didn't leave?" we ask.

Oh, just for the holiday. Life goes on.

Plucks a fig.

Tell Stories

Somebody swindled somebody. Somebody did C-sections on pregnant soldiers on a battlefield, watching instructions on YouTube. Somebody rescued someone.

Those two fought every day for sixty years. But they were good fights.

Experience mounds on experience.

Mount of Olives. Mount of Beatitudes. *Jesus walked here. Jesus taught here.*

Here is the route Jesus took. This is the only way Jesus could come.

They knew him. They loved him. They hated him.

He had friends in high places. Magdalene was likely rich in this wealthy town of Magdala. Likely hired Jesus for carpentry.

Remains of the synagogue. Patches of fresco. Jesus taught here, where the parables live.

The First Temple. The Second Temple. The Destruction of the Temple. The agony in the garden. The agony of everyone. Tumbled stones of the Temple, heaped here two thousand years.

Tunnels under the Temple. Mysterious, tremendous bus-sized building-block of solid stone at the base of the Western Wall.

Pray Tell

The Western Wall above, where under the golden dome the pigeons swoop the golden stone.

The need to pray is great.

The self who prays listens.

The wall hums.

is there room for my prayer what if there's no space, no time to poke my paper in if I share my prayer will it not come true please please please thank you

Selfies, forbidden at the Western Wall, are snapped anyway: a shoulder shows, a mirror drops. Even the vain pray. Even the brash.

Wall warms the palms: *it's moving   breathing like a living animal what if there's no time no space*

Now move aside. The need to pray is great. That pigeon wants that shady place that other pigeon has.

Experience mounds on experience

Sail the Sea of Galilee. Wade among curious fish. Nearby, apostles raised their nets groaning with Christ-foretold bounty.

Messiah. Has He come? Will He come? Is this He?

Sumptuous hummus. Such labneh. Fig pomegranate date grape olive wheat barley.

Mohammed climbed this rock and was lifted by Ariel. *The Dome of the Rock is a shrine, not a mosque.*

Sundown. Three stars. New Day.

No river, no sea near Jerusalem. Flow not easy. Hills and valleys hard to cross.

Donkeys made it possible. Slaves made it possible. Herod made it possible.

Here at his hidden gate is probably where Pilate stood. And where we stand, the crowd cried for Barabbas.

Built around the bony stone of Golgotha and the tomb that Constantine declared belonged to Christ, the Church of the Holy Sepulchre.

On Holy Saturday each year for the "Miracle" of Holy Fire, twenty thousand gather in the single-exit church, holding fists of burning candles. Hair on fire sometimes, passion, weeping, screams for God, carrying flames home on special flights to Orthodox Greece, Serbia, Bulgaria.

Our guide indicates the probably real tomb, unadorned but for an unlit oil lamp one of us backs into, splattering blessings.

Plazas. Quarters. Blocks. Building blocks. City on top of city on top of city time jumping constantly. The present is the core sample.

Truth Tells

They shoot that building on the hill for Bethlehem on
Christmas cards.

Christians make up 1 percent here. Only twelve
thousand Believers.

Banksy his hotel: "The Walled-off Astoria" overlooking the
West Bank Wall at Bethlehem, where it is not Christmas cards
they shoot.

Security cameras and slingshots mounted on the bar wall like
trophy animals;

a mural of Israeli and Palestinian soldiers pillowfighting.

You can go to Jericho but only on a bus.

City of Gates: Zion Gate New Gate Herod's Gate Dung Gate
Lions Gate Gate of Damascus. Jaffa's a Gate and a breach in
the wall made for an emperor's entrance. The Gate of Mercy is
blocked, awaiting The Messiah and the resurrected dead.

The Gate of Mercy is blocked.

You must join us. You cannot join us. You don't deserve
to join us.

I will not look at you. I must not look at you. Get out of
here. Come in.

Bright wares. Dark markets. Blinding stone. Heaps of greens,
figs, fake Oreos: plareos, sugar incense dung battered peeling
paint sky flags weapons. Arms in young arms.

Covered women. Women covered. *Do not look at me. I cannot*
look at you.

Antiquities: the widow's mite now available in shops. Animals dance on Armenian pottery.

In your business. In your face. Checking his papers. Bumping into her. Deliberately.

Screeching brinking schoolgirls flitting. Booming boys bounce down stairs.

Please. Stay with tour.

Pure and lovely voice singing Ladino, Yiddish at table.

Sundown. Three stars. New Day.

Tiles Tell

This land is no mosaic where elements can be removed and still a picture seen.

Look underfoot. Tiles tell. In this land, by design, throbbing cruciforms recede to daisies, daisies blossom into crosses back to daisies, black and white eternally whiching, switching. Ancient patterns. Both/none dominant   neither ignored   no either /or. Not picture. Pattern. Both.

Sundown. Three stars. New Day.

But the Babylonians. But the Assyrians. But the Romans. But the Crusaders. But the Ottomans. But the British. But the Israelis. But the Palestinians. But the Israelis. But the Palestinians.

The circle and the star. The underlying patterns.

But the cups of tea. But the babies. But the bread. The dates. The wine. The smoke. The greens. The weavings. The hanging meat. The sparkling fish. The raucous laughter. The drums. The music. Clapping rhythm. Shofar.

Sundown. Three stars. New day.

Self As Tell

Slipping under consciousness, lifetime piles up. Shards surface. Bright memories. Whole events. We are guests.

Sundown. Three stars. New day.

There are no gates to heaven.

Sympathies

Broken Just So

Sad events have happened recently, not so much to me directly, but in the lives of people close to people close to me. Business disappointments, unexpected hospitalizations and the untimely passing of a young mother here in our community darkened many hearts.

What do we make of such pains, such losses? A treasured vase came to mind. It belonged to my mother and is an object whose graceful fanning fluted form I have ever loved. Earlier this year it broke.

It did not shatter, but it will never hold water and a live bouquet again. Yet I couldn't bring myself to throw it out. I kept it in my studio with the broken places turned from view. This morning I was inspired to take a little action and refrain from cursing the darkness, so to speak. Because it had broken just so, I could thread a small bulb on a simple a fixture precisely through the break.

Had the break not been just so, this lovely glowing lamp would not exist. But neither would it exist had the break never happened.

Let us hope that in those times life breaks our hearts, they break just so. To let our light shine forth.

A Phrase to Melt Anxiety

I'm fidgeting in the car service sedan, rushing to LaGuardia
thanks to the overslept driver. (Never book a flight on July 5
and expect a young driver to forgo celebration the night before.
Perhaps March 18 and May 6 are not so good either.)

I am anxious about making my flight, when suddenly I remind
myself that this is an act of love. The motivation for this trip is
to visit my sisters: an act of love; and to support my husband
in his latest endeavor: another act of love. It's a phrase that has
occurred to me before, and it always relaxes me.

It did not mean I caught the plane. I didn't. I missed it by a few
moments and took my place in line at the ticket agent. The man
in front of me was furious at missing the same flight, and let
loose on the agent, who was unable to get him aboard it. The
man stomped off to file a complaint.

But an act of love always involves the larger energy, which
means we can relax. With this in mind, I was able to be humane
with the agent. Turns out he gets up every morning at 1:30 to
get to the airport by 3:30, when his shift starts. (Even a bit of
personal concern for another human being is relaxing.) After
a brief conversation, I was on the next flight out, no doubt
before the angry man had finished filing his complaint. And the
grateful agent flagged my luggage triple priority.

Thanks to my unexpected layover in Houston, I ended a
ridiculously long search for the perfect denim jacket. While I
missed a few hours with my sister, I got there by day's end.

It's an act of love. Relax.

Let's remember how many of our daily acts hold this motivation—answering an email, picking up a child from school, trying to finish a project which helps support those we love. Our lives are filled with acts of love.

The more acts of love we recognize, the more relaxed we get to be.

A Wish for Any Wedding

One day last month, while eating a bowl of oatmeal, I slit the inside of my lip.

I felt that infantile fury, shock and unfairness we feel when pain comes out of nowhere, when all ordinary precautions of life have been taken, yet something goes awry. Whole-grain danger? In our very mouths? Looking at the spoon itself, I understood.

Almost forty years ago yesterday, on our wedding day, nestled in a chest with the rest of the set, sat this soup spoon, brand-new. We decided not to save our silver "for good," but to use it every day. Thirty years spooning oatmeal, chili, soup with this spoon. Thirty years soaping and rinsing and wiping it dry.

I realized we have lived together long enough to wear down our spoons. What cut me was the glorious thinning edge of commitment.

In its capacity to deliver both nourishment and pain, marriage is a knife-edged spoon. But as the gauze of years unwinds, as intention and love become more refined, marriage becomes the inverse of the spoon that bit me.

The knife-edge dulls, subsides to mere accident, like a scratch of your spouse's unclipped nail. The measure of the bowl expands and deepens, holding and offering health, awareness, joy. A spoon that shines even when empty.

My love and I celebrate many sterling decades of spooning together. While marriage may not be for everyone, we can't help congratulating and encouraging all the young couples

we meet. We've become our own proverb—a wish for a long
marriage: May your spoons grow thin in your mouths.

My mind's like a sieve.

It catches what's important.

Soulgrowing

Sagrada Familia is the colorful, starry-pinnacled, unfinished basilica whose towers grace many a Barcelona guidebook. It was designed by Antoni Gaudi, and the photos I'd seen made me think his work quirky. Novel, but arbitrary. Travel throws my ignorance in high relief, and thereby grows my soul.

The exterior is indeed colorful, syncopated, idiosyncratic, but for now, step out of the hot Spanish noon through the massive bronze doors into cool dim, which in a moment opens on a silver grove dappled with light: golden and white and the rotating wheel of the spectrum.

You are in a spiritual translation of a forest. In this shapely generous space, stone trunks rise, twist, branch, uphold a curved and jagged honeycomb of sky. At one end, through Gaudi's mastery of mathematics, construction, light, design, and materials, saturated in his love of his work, of nature and of his divine "Client," he translates the sun for us. It becomes the very Eye of God, and unlike our sun, we can look into it.

Free of cliché, of visual dogma. "This interior gives me faith in the future of human spirituality," I whisper to John. Fresh, harmonic, flexible. Room for souls to grow.

Gaudi began work on the basilica 1883 and completed but a quarter of his design in his lifetime. He was at peace. "My client is not in a hurry," he said.

Work continues in order to complete it by 2026, the centennial of the architect's death.

We'll just have to play it

by heart.

Geographies

The Limitless Within

Carlsbad Caverns

Ride a sardine elevator to a depth the height of the Empire
State Building. Exit. Enter the dim cool hushed umber passage.
Delta into the Big Room. Halt. Jaw. Gigantic. As if an open.

Inert. Eyes expand. Vast. As if. Massive draping stones.
Tablecloth. Feel again a child. Crystal vestments. Stone sails.
Step. Body. Having one. Shift beyond the exploded grammar
of experience.

Hollows horns spears spires. Dream but it is Earth. Also Art.
Symphonic shapes. Forms like carved jade forests, temples,
baroque theatres. Rutted bark, rippled dunes, knobbed
mollusks, sandsilk cheek.

Sulfuric acid etches with abandon, colors with restraint. Coffee
tea parchment dust ebony sienna mud. Overhead, underfoot:
the elegant discipline of sepia.

Overheard: only murmurs, sharing awe, silence, accord.
Underground silences and darkens phones, slows and
hushes voices.

Salinity. Serenity.

Still, secretly the eye seeks edges, borders, tries to contain this
intricate immensity, to grasp the evaporating self. An ocean is
simplicity. The stars are but themselves, but within the within,
there is no edge. Or rather, multitudes of edges each unique,
infinitely opening into opening: crevices cavities holes pocks
pricks pits.

Brain, chest, imagination open into opening as pupils dilate to their utmost in utmost darkness. Limitless withinning.

Circumambulating this colossal chamber takes an hour.

Tomorrow, with guides and gloves and helmets, reach the Lower Cave by rope and ladders lit by bouncing headlamps. Beware slick spots. Adrenalin rushing like sulfuric acid, carving new muscular awareness. Wonder how trembling is supposed to help. No matter no waver of attention when risk is high. The body's strength and care deliver the riches of this fewly-entered space: patience time water again again the ancient sea, again her limestone her tiny shells, again the whimsy and gravitas of process.

Turn off your headlamps, says the guide. Plunge into ultimate darkness.

Consider Jim White, a youth with a torch and a taste for the dark, who, tracking the ascension of a million bats, found this limitless within in 1898. Came back again and again, knowing the inner pathless world is not an empty thing.

Give it presence, light, curiosity. A few feet at a time.

Pools, pits, ledges abound. Find safety in focus. In safety find splendor.

Later on a lantern tour, by candlelight with awestruck children and their parents, see it as Jim did: soft shadows caressing the wordless forms, the glittering folds, the tusks the domes, the droppings of stone. Carpets of cave pearls, each formed when drops of moving water coat a tiny grit with calcite, coating and turning it, coating and turning it, playful as oysters, shaping stone pills, bubbling jawbreakers over the floor. And more.

Time to return. Ignore the elevator. Take the natural passage.

Upward through utterly different forms: theatrical, thorny,
bony, pocked and peppered surfaces. Mammoth jutting
pelvises. Gothic buttresses. Suddenly: climbing Blake's very
ladder, spiraling through magnificent Within within us all,
resplendent, spiraling upward out of the earth, through dreamy
cathedrals up to the glimpses of sunlight, the chirping claims of
swooping swallows crisscrossing the widening entrance. Pass
the holy cloisters of the sleeping million bats, out upward from
the cool steady clean cave air into the slam and suck of surface
heat, light so slappingly bright...incomprehensible: the sun as a
daily companion.

Glad to Be Human

a joie de coeur

Glad to Be Human

Glad to be human in the twentieth-first century, survival licked, glad not to be selling my blood anymore or using rolled-up toilet paper for sanitary napkins. But even in those dollar-few days, I'd find a bunch of roses abandoned on the street, or once, walking up Eighth Avenue to meet my date, the strap to my only pair of shoes disintegrated and I went into a hotel after three barefoot blocks and said, "Do you have any shoes?" and they did, a pair of Dr. Scholl's that someone left that fit just right. Glad to be human, glad to be provided for, glad to provide for myself in faith and effort. Fun to find shoes, fun to buy them, too.

◇◇◇

Glad to be human—for solitude and to be able to be a stranger—a gift of the twenty-first century, like speed and music anytime and feast upon feast of stories anytime. Glad to be human for late nights, talk and art and sex and loving and all different languages, glad to be human for words themselves, peculiar to us as paper to the wasp, as leaf to tree or song to bird; words, as human as a measured square.

◇◇◇

Glad to be human in the twenty-first century, where people spend lives designing, dancing, building, writing, studying their minutest fascinations, people dedicating lives to food or fashion or philosophy, creating and creating, absorbed in their work for love of it, as now they marry for love. People hungering to understand each other and their families, reading, talking, tending the earth and their dreams, and the playing of games and of sport.

◇◇◇

Glad in the twenty-first century of all the mighty banquets
laid: images of art of all our centuries reproduced and held in
hand, writings of the writing cultures held in heart, spiritual
traditions of the ages spread before us: choose, sample,
compare, enjoy, discard, invent from the immense library
of remembered human life! Deep feeding of consciousness.
History lies on the bed, saying take me, take all you wish of me,
and then leave me behind, I don't mind.

◇◇◇

Glad to be human for the feasts of all cuisines, any day any
taste in the world and invented combinations, like discovered
common tastes in conversations between strangers, the mixing
of cultures complementing the glorious rush of fruit and
vegetable and grain, fresh and fresh, glad.

◇◇◇

Glad to be human for the knowledge of animals and nature
and material and metal and chemistry and theory, living in a
living dictionary of experience and interest and curiosity, glad
to know some things about my human body, of her cells and
structures, glad to know about some stars, glad the mystery is
infinite, glad for the burst and silence.

◇◇◇

Glad to be living in the heart, the human heart, time for whole
days spent on relationships, for soothing, for expressing pain,
for pleasure, contemplation. And time and ways and means for
distant friends, living in differing places, to visit, to speak and
the beauty of a letter sent received.

◇◇◇

Glad for interiors and colors and pattern and balance and
shape and movement and adornment and the way the future
vapors on a loom. Glad of myriads of little helps, of zippers,
paperclips, and cleverness. And of the explicit agreement in
ongoing ordinary existence of plate glass.

◇◇◇

Glad of the beauty of stones and their wisdoms, grandmothers
of matter; glad of all the world, how much wider, fuller, more
colorful can it be? The wild harmonic variation, rushes of
beauty from all cultures differing, flood of beauty, glad to be
here for this!

Glad to be safe and dry and educated and supplied and
empowered and free of children, glad there are people glad to
have children. Glad to choose, to help to nourish, to bless.

◇◇◇

Glad to have coached a baby into this world, excruciating and
exquisite. No sleep for twenty-four hours, my sister twisting
in the birthing bed, her husband and me squeezing her hand,
feeding her ice, our very breaths as one till salty weepy laughter
chokes out of us as the red hairy head appears.

◇◇◇

Glad to be human for all the ages that surround me always, for
the precious ability always to catch sight of a baby somewhere,
a toddler and children, and the sweet pure unconsciousness of,
even in anger, youth, staggering in its unknowing beauty. And
the reposed beauty of lined faces, relaxing into life, tendered
by experience, the comfort of the presence of wisdom, with

vigor yet, a beauty like a leatherbound book. And the grace of
elders realized in full capacity, inspiring as centuries-old trees,
the crowning loveliness of natures fulfilled, experience like
rings around them of their growth, not separate into years,
these feelings, but sensed around them as a life, a single mighty
sheath of living over their ordinary comings and goings, sap
rising and falling in them in thin streams, surrounded by the
immensity of their truth.

◇◇◇

Glad to have helped at death as well, not only the slow dangle
from the hospital tubes for those I knew, but for the stranger,
the old man dying alone on the southeast corner of 42nd Street
and Ninth Avenue in NYC, to crouch at his crumpled barely
moving body, hold his colding hand, tell him he did a good job
with life, to feel his spirit lighten and leave, like a bird.

◇◇◇

Glad to see the old ones with the young ones, and the middles
with them both, embracing the holy hidden web, the knowledge
at once forward and backward, the intentions of youth, the
obligations of middleage, the liberations of age. Joys at every
stage and moment, at no time without memory, at no time
without expectation, life at once like a film in a can. Much
gladness that we share this, reminding each other over and over
with alphabets of behavior and emotion, familiar and combined
to sentences newly every day.

And glad to be human for the sake of days, that all of human
history has taken place in days. The Battle of Hastings
happened on a day, and so did the dancing of Fred Astaire, and
all of us have days for all emotion, exploration, for being sick,
recovering from travel, gathering with friends, holidays, and

days for being bored, for recreation and creation, days and days and infinite days.

◇◇◇

Glad to be human for cooking and slicing life, looking for meaning and searching and finding the missing word, the lost sock, the thrilly scary moment reaching around in your purse and not finding your wallet, rummaging, rummaging, knowing it's there, finding it under your fingers with pleasure, and finding with pleasure at last that the meaning of life's like a cell on the field of your vision, you know it is there, but each time you look it springs out of your sight, but looking at anything else, it springs back into place and you're looking right through it. Glad to be human, abundantly answered

◇◇◇

Hard to see the effort behind abundance, here in the early twenty-first century: the spent backs picking berries, raw red nursing hands, the sweat of science, years of boredom for a single thought; hard to see the editor tossing in her sleep, the relentless raising of children, the grinding of wheat, the servicing of machinery, but when I am spent and raw with sweat and sleeplessness working my work asking how can it be so hard, I remember what work it takes to bring me any single thing. My gladness of all I am brought begets gratitude, and gratitude lightens my service. And all becomes service and gladness and gratitude.

◇◇◇

Glad for the transformations now and coming, glad for love and work and play, glad for letting go my fear to sound my song of gladness, going as it does against prevailing currents in the thinkers of my day. Glad I learned the joy of swimming against the current in a Catskill cataract. Full strength deliberate infinity swimming, whole self pleasure challenge, young lad paddles over asking, "Do you know you're not going anywhere?" and me yessing and loving the power of current, power of body, free from having to watch where I'm going, free from having to turn around or curb my body from a pool wall, a pond curve, free from "Am I going out too far?" in salt and bobbing water, free to swim and nothing else with all myself and a man swims over, says, "You're fighting the current," and "No," I say, "I'm enjoying it!" Whole self, full power, glad to be human.

Afterword

Glad to Be Human: Adventures in Optimism takes
the reader on an honest and joyful journey exploring what it
means to be alive and present in the world today. Eloquent,
thoughtful, inviting prose as well as the intimate moments the
author shares of her own observations about being human,
inspire one to be better at it (being human) and serve to remind
us of the power of gratitude, optimism and faith.

Irene's words, whether painting a picture of her first
experiences in Paris, of a walk south in NYC after the
unthinkable tragedy of 9/11 or in contemplating creativity,
writing and gardening, push the reader to think about who they
are in the world and how they want to be. One sees through her
eyes that even the small, unexpected things, like a stinging bite
from a caterpillar when repotting neglected houseplants, can
serve to heighten our senses and make us glad to be human.
The masterfully crafted words interwoven between essays,
like the chime of a Tibetan singing bowl, resonate and linger
with you and move you to a new way of seeing and being.
The simplicity of her words gives us much to contemplate
when expressed in such thoughts as "We All Become Masters
at Expressing Ourselves" and "There is Always Time if You
Do It Now."

Knowing Irene as a friend and fellow bookwoman is truly one
of the things that I am grateful for in my own life and it is
wonderful to know that through this book, others will have the
opportunity to learn from, and be inspired by, her marvelous
way of being. As she reminds us so beautifully in this book, the
power of viewing even the most mundane or difficult things in

our lives as "acts of love," including how we treat each other, can provide the optimism we need to find peace in the world. This book is truly a gift for anyone in need of feeling connected, hopeful and human.

Jane Kinney Denning
Acquisitions Editor Mango Media, Inc.
Immediate Past President of the Women's National Book Association
WNBA Representative to the United Nations Department of Global Communication/Civil Society Unit

Acknowledgements

Warmest thanks to my beloved and steadfast agent, Anne Marie O'Farrell, whose belief in my work continues to get me out of the kitchen and back to the desk. It's been a pleasure to work with my editor Alexandra Franzen who created this delightful Tiny Books imprint. I offer special gratitude to the sweet and savvy associate publisher Brenda Knight, who suggested this book to me. Her support of my work has been a treasured beacon lighting my path. Thanks also to publisher Chris McKenney, designer Jayoung Hong, and all the Mango team who helped distribute this tidy volume.

Particular and enduring gratitude to Bill Henderson and the Pushcart Prize editors who selected the essay that gave this collection its title and spirit, with special appreciation to editor Wayne Thomas who first published it in *The Tusculum Review*. Profound thanks to the other journals and anthologies who first published essays found in this book. Anyone who reads or runs a literary magazine helps keep writers alive. Thanks to the small but mighty organizations: the Butterfield Library in Cold Spring, NY, the Desmond Fish Library in Garrison, Calling All Poets in New Paltz, NY, and Poets and Writers in NYC, who continue to create space for writers to share their work.

Writing thrives on friendship. For years of wonderful conversations and support, thank you to Jean Marzollo (sorely missed) and to Patricia Adams. Dear Tracy Strong, here I am thanking you again for gabfests, cheerleading and heart-to-hearts. Gratitude to dear Mark Lacko, for design expertise, headshots, brimming bowls of garden produce and for mending my dictionary stand and other irreplaceables. Thomas Donahue, you and beloved Mark Rettman are an unending source of inspiration, kindness and laughter. Thanks, Bill and Ann Strohmeier, for your great senses of humor and perspective.

Thank you for the juicy talks, literary and otherwise, dear Ed McCann and Richard Kollath. Your creation Read650: Where Writers Read is a gift to writers and audiences alike.

I'll always be grateful to Laura Shaine Cunningham, who, with her signature kindness and wisdom, helped me turn an important literary corner. Thanks to all my supportive sibs and their spouses and offsprings.

Heidi, Michael and Astrid Bender, you have changed our lives with our cherished Split Rock Books. Long may you reign in Cold Spring and beyond!

Robin O'Brien, how many different ways can I think up to thank you? A challenge I will gleefully undertake for the rest of our lives. For now, take these specific thanks for our hilarious, necessary Sunday phonecalls and for your spirit, support and equanimity. John, darling John, John Pielmeier, the daily bread of your love sustains me. You are one of my gladdest reasons to be human and our million-year marriage is a beautiful edifice of devotion I will always be proud of and grateful for.

And thank you, Mother Nature, for everything.

Publication Credits

"A Visit to Liberty" (*Hawaii Pacific Review*)

"An Argument with Water" *(decomP*, Read650: *The Great Outdoors*)

"City of Strings" (Zone 3)

"Glad to Be Human" (*The Tusculum Review, The Pushcart Prize Anthology XXXVI*)

"Tell of Israel" (*Caveat Lector*)

"The Smudge Between Stars" (*Fjords Review*)

"Walking South" (*Confrontation*)

"Taking the Plunge" (*Thresholds Quarterly*)

"The Birthing Tent" (*Apalachee Review*)

"The Cookie Crumbles" (*Midway*)

About the Author

Irene O'Garden has won or been nominated for prizes in nearly every writing category from stage to e-screen, hardcovers, and children's books as well as literary magazines and anthologies. Her critically-acclaimed play *Women On Fire* (Samuel French), starring Judith Ivey, played sold-out houses at Off-Broadway's Cherry Lane Theatre and was nominated for a Lucille Lortel Award. Her latest play, *Little Heart*, about artist Corita Kent, won her a Berilla Kerr Playwriting Fellowship and was awarded full development at the New Harmony Play Project.

O'Garden was awarded a Pushcart Prize for her lyric essay "Glad to Be Human," included in this volume. Harper published her first memoir *Fat Girl*, and Nirala Press published her book *Fulcrum: Selected Poems*, which contains her prize-winning poem "Nonfiction." "Morning Coffee" won the Scott Meyer Award. Her poems and essays have been featured in dozens of literary journals and award-winning anthologies (including *A Slant of Light*, USA Best Book Award for Anthology), and she has been honored with an Alice Desmond Award and an Oppenheimer for her children's books.

O'Garden has appeared at top literary venues including The Player's Club, The National Arts Club, the Bowery Poetry Club, Nuyorican Poetry Café, and KGB in Manhattan; The Poetry Café, Mycennae House and Vinyl Deptford in London, and in Jerusalem. She's a regular contributor to *650: Where Writers Read*, in Manhattan and Sarah Lawrence College and has received several grants from Poets & Writers. O'Garden has lived joyfully with her husband John Pielmeier, for forty years. Most known for his play *Agnes of God*, John also writes movies, miniseries, and novels (*Hook's Tale*, Scribner). His stage adaptation of *The Exorcist* ran in London's West End and Mexico City and toured the UK. Plans to bring it to New York City are in the works.

What makes you Glad to Be Human?

Head to

www.gladtobehuman.com

to see what others have said

and add a thought of your own!

Mango Publishing, established in 2014, publishes an eclectic list of books by diverse authors—both new and established voices—on topics ranging from business, personal growth, women's empowerment, LGBTQ studies, health, and spirituality to history, popular culture, time management, decluttering, lifestyle, mental wellness, aging, and sustainable living. We were recently named 2019's #1 fastest growing independent publisher by *Publishers Weekly*. Our success is driven by our main goal, which is to publish high quality books that will entertain readers as well as make a positive difference in their lives.

Our readers are our most important resource; we value your input, suggestions, and ideas. We'd love to hear from you—after all, we are publishing books for you!

Please stay in touch with us and follow us at:

Facebook: Mango Publishing

Twitter: @MangoPublishing

Instagram: @MangoPublishing

LinkedIn: Mango Publishing

Pinterest: Mango Publishing

Sign up for our newsletter at www.mangopublishinggroup.com and receive a free book!

Join us on Mango's journey to reinvent publishing, one book at a time.

CPSIA information can be obtained
at www.ICGtesting.com
Printed in the USA
JSHW021242281120
9839JS00004B/4